American Infanticide

Critical Issues in Crime and Society

Raymond J. Michalowski and Luis A. Fernandez, Series Editors

Critical Issues in Crime and Society is oriented toward critical analysis of contemporary problems in crime and justice. The series is open to a broad range of topics including specific types of crime, wrongful behavior by economically or politically powerful actors, controversies over justice system practices, and issues related to the intersection of identity, crime, and justice. It is committed to offering thoughtful works that will be accessible to scholars and professional criminologists, general readers, and students.

For a complete list of titles in the series, please see the last page of the book.

American Infanticide

Sexism, Science, and the Politics of Sympathy

Clara S. Lewis

RUTGERS UNIVERSITY PRESS
NEW BRUNSWICK, CAMDEN, AND NEWARK, NEW JERSEY
LONDON AND OXFORD

Rutgers University Press is a department of Rutgers, The State University of New Jersey, one of the leading public research universities in the nation. By publishing worldwide, it furthers the University's mission of dedication to excellence in teaching, scholarship, research, and clinical care.

Library of Congress Cataloging-in-Publication Data

Names: Lewis, Clara S., 1981– author
Title: American infanticide : sexism, science, and the politics of sympathy / Clara S. Lewis.
Description: New Brunswick : Rutgers University Press, 2025. | Series: Critical issues in crime and society | Includes bibliographical references and index. | Identifiers: LCCN 2024047714 | ISBN 9781978833821 paperback | ISBN 9781978833838 hardcover | ISBN 9781978833845 epub | ISBN 9781978833869 pdf
Subjects: LCSH: Infanticide—United States—History | Women—United States—Social conditions | Motherhood—Social aspects—United States
Classification: LCC HV6541.U6 L49 2025 | DDC 304.6/68—dc23/eng/20250306
LC record available at https://lccn.loc.gov/2024047714

A British Cataloging-in-Publication record for this book is available from the British Library.

rutgersuniversitypress.org

For Addison Grace Weaver and all the unknown babies born into death

Contents

American Infanticide

Introduction

"DISGRACED BY A CRIME SO DISGUSTING"

Harter Cemetery in Hannibal, Ohio, looks more like a sledding hill than a final resting place. The narrow yard with a handful of graves sits directly above the Ohio River, overlooking West Virginia. Along this stretch of the river, elegant twentieth-century steel railway bridges rust above newly laid pipelines. The landscape splits between active coal mines, oil and gas extraction plants, and forested hillsides overrun by white-tailed deer. Billboards next to the interstate read, "Drug traffickers go to prison," "Salvation is free, Jesus already paid," and "Lion's Den Adult Super Store."

At the highest point in the cemetery, baby Addison Grace Weaver's headstone overlooks a football field at the high school her mother, Emile (pronounced "Emily") Louise Weaver, attended. Carved neatly into the headstone's polished black marble, white letters read: "Our Little Angel, April 22, 2015–April 22, 2015." White with dark brown hair, Addison weighed just shy of seven pounds at birth. The color of her eyes is unknown. The headstone for Addison's step-great-grandfather, Lonnie Potts (1940–2010), lies thirty feet to the right. Nothing but close-cut grass occupies the space between the two graves. The Potts family owns a total of fifteen grave sites between Lonnie and Addison. Born into death, Addison arrived at Harter two generations before her time.

Seventy-five miles west of the cemetery on the campus of Muskingum University in New Concord, Ohio, Addison was delivered into a toilet in a closet-sized bathroom in the Delta sorority house. She likely perished minutes after birth either in the toilet bowl or in a garbage bag as Emile, a sophomore with no medical training, cleaned up the bathroom where she had labored in silence and alone.

News of Addison's demise went viral. Emile's case was reported on locally before she had even received postpartum medical treatment and globally during her trial. She was featured in *People* and *Elle* magazines and is one of the subjects of the documentary *Baby Doe*. Tabloids and teen magazines published selfies Emile had taken in the months prior to the birth, dolled up with her Delta sorority sisters, and tracked every nagging detail of the case against her. Emile was condemned for the cheap flask of whiskey in her dorm room, the half-empty bottle of herbal black cohosh pills, and the rough game of dodgeball she played during Greek Week with her baby bump visible from the bleachers.

These scandalous details made it easy for the local prosecutor and reporters to strip Emile of her individual identity and label her a monster mom. The *Daily News* reported, "Former Ohio college student killed hours-old newborn, left her in the trash outside sorority house";[1] *The Washington Post*, quoting a text message from Emile to her ex-boyfriend that was presented during her trial, wrote, "'No more baby': Sorority sister gets life term for tossing newborn into trash to die";[2] *The U.S. Sun* led with "Killer's Regret: Sorority girl jailed for life after 'throwing her newborn baby in the TRASH' now feels like a monster."[3] The rhetoric of these headlines, especially the active verb choices, mirror the prosecutor's argument that Emile concealed her pregnancy with homicidal intent, then purposefully killed Addison by "throwing" and "tossing" her in the trash. The headlines validated the prosecutor's decision to charge Emile with aggravated murder, the jury's decision to convict, and the judge's insistence on handing Emile the maximum possible sentence for her first criminal offense.

During the sentencing hearing at the end of her trial, the judge condemned Emile for being "selfish" and "callous." Emile's punishment was explicitly justified by what the judge viewed as her failure to express maternal affection and selflessness. These attributes and the stereotype of maternity to which they adhere trace back to British common law and Puritan sermons. How did these myths about the nature of motherhood retain relevance 300 years later? How might we understand Emile and Addison's tragedy differently without resorting to stereotypes about monster moms to explain her motive?

Few infant homicide cases are reported on nationally. Yet these tragedies are not a rare, or even surprising, occurrence. The homicide rate for babies, children, and teenagers is consistently higher in the United States than much of the rest of the world: the most recent United Nations report on U.S. homicide rates documented 5.3 infant and child homicides per 100,000 people in the United States, compared to 0.6 per 100,000 in Europe.[4] In terms of infant homicides more narrowly, the most recent Centers for Disease Control and Prevention (CDC) report based on data from 2017 to 2020 identified 1,067 total cases in which a baby was killed during the first year of life. More than half of these killings occurred during the postpartum period.[5]

Very few of these tragedies gain national, or even local, attention. Despite the cultural fascination with monster moms like Emile, the majority of known contemporary cases of infant homicide appear to be committed accidentally by men during episodes of violent physical abuse.[6] A rare, recent study examining infant homicide cases reported by the National Violent Injury Statistics System found that sixty-five out of seventy-two cases were perpetrated by men who were either the baby's father or the boyfriend of the mother. The researchers note that most of these tragedies were "impulsive," "unintended" attacks during which the father or boyfriend either beat or shook the infant to death. The study further finds that these murders were not the first incident of physical abuse committed against the baby victim.[7] Stories about babies that die as a result of abuse and neglect, however, are too sad to sell. There's little vicarious moral relief to be gained when parents who are grieving or enduring crisis are punished. There's even less appetite for a serious evidence-based evaluation of many Americans' long-standing preference for physically punitive parenting methods.

While the majority of infant homicide cases are invisible, high-profile monster mom trials have been blockbusters since the colonial era, with thousands traveling great distances to view the public hangings of women convicted of infanticide on Boston Common and listen to their final confessions. These public spectacles incite disgust at a mother who reacts to her baby's vulnerability with callous self-interest instead of altruistic affection. This book calls attention to everything this morality tale—which has been retold almost verbatim since the colonial era—omits. The mother's life circumstances are irrelevant to this kind of monster mom discourse; the influence of family, friends, and male partners as well as the pressures exerted by social values, cultural norms, and religious dictates are left out of the narrative. The equally significant circumstances of conception, which might include rape or incest or infidelity, are omitted. These stories also neglect the subtle reality of pregnancy recognition, a complex, multistep process full of ambiguities that are meaningful for many women, not a facile yes or no test,[8] and do not account for the mitigating medical impact of unassisted childbirth or the potentially mitigating mental health impacts of the postpartum period. In essence, popular stories about monster moms and dumpster babies serve sentiment and stereotype over an accurate account of the medical, social, and cultural factors that drive these recurring tragedies.

When these highly relevant contexts are omitted from public consideration, bias and inconsistency dictate how women accused of infant homicide are perceived and punished. In but one telling example of this incoherence, two years after Emile's conviction, another young woman named Brooke Skylar Richardson was charged with aggravated murder and gross abuse of a corpse in Ohio for the death and improper burial of her newborn infant daughter, Annabel. The CBS special about the case was the number one non-sports primetime program the Saturday it aired, attracting an audience of 3.33 million viewers. Stories like Brooke's and Emile's become newsworthy when they include shocking details about violence done to the infant's corpse or the accused mother's lifestyle. These narratives create dramatic tension by inviting audiences to assess the young women's culpability—politicizing sympathy to justify either lenience or harsh punishment.

After laboring silently and alone in a downstairs bathroom, Brooke, then in her senior year of high school, buried Annabel at the back of her family's yard. Ashes were found on Annabel's corpse when it was discovered two months after the burial; an expert working for the state suggested that the ashes were evidence that Brooke had attempted to cremate the body. Brooke's legal team raised doubts about the quality of the state's forensic analysis, arguing that Brooke had taken charred flowers from her prom, which had been disposed of on her family's backyard grill, and placed them lovingly with Annabel's corpse while burying her. They also pointed to the interrogating police officers' manipulative tactics; a female officer held Brooke's hand tenderly during her initial interview, appearing to empathize with her ordeal, while another officer recorded her confession.

In the 2019 special on the CBS program *48 Hours*, titled "The Case Against Brooke Skylar Richardson," Brooke's father was interviewed in his large, sunny kitchen with the family's well-groomed Miniature Schnauzer underfoot and advocated movingly on her behalf. During the special and the televised trial, Brooke remained silent and appeared dangerously emaciated. The narrative presented by her representatives emphasized her severe eating disorder and redirected blame at her mother, casting Brooke convincingly as both a "daddy's girl" and a victim while leading many to conclude that her baby had been stillborn. Brooke served seven days in jail. Her probation was terminated early after she made a statement about "suffering in silence" and being ready to show that she was capable of "being a normal person again."[9]

Emile, by contrast, lacked effective legal counsel and a male advocate with status to speak up on her behalf. Her biological father, a Vietnam War veteran, died when she was eleven. In the years before Emile left for college, her stepfather did not fully accept her presence among his children—labeling his food as off-limits to her and requesting that she not "dent" his couch. Alone during her trial, Emile was the only person called upon to testify in her defense.

Research demonstrates what is evident in the contrast between how Brooke's and Emily's tragedies were punished: that the American legal system and press distort motives and ignore contexts to place women who are accused of killing their offspring into one of three categories—evil, insane, or victim[10]—and assign blame accordingly. Pitied as a victim, Brooke was found innocent. Condemned as evil, Emile's first opportunity for parole will arise only after she serves twenty years of her life sentence.

Misrepresentation not only breeds biased, inconsistent applications of the law but also undermines our ability to make sense of the scale of infant homicide risk, which is more widespread than many realize. By containing risk in an identifiable other, stories about monster moms obscure an alarming reality known to researchers but missing from public discourse: contemporary infanticide is a vestige, not an aberration. Aberration is defined as "a departure from an ethical or behavioral standard; a deviation from what is normal, usual, or expected, typically an unwelcome one."[11] Infanticides that garner news media coverage tend to be salacious and shocking, thus reinforcing the assumption that these tragedies are rare. A vestige, in contrast, is a remnant of our evolutionary past: "a surviving memorial or trace of some condition, quality, practice, serving as an indication of its former existence; a surviving trace of some part formerly existing in the species."[12] The wings of a penguin, no longer used to fly but still useful for navigation and balance under water, are a vestige. Infanticide, once an evolutionary necessity, is a vestige, a possibility for any parent in crisis.

The extensive history of infanticide in the West has only recently come to light. Yet a careful reading of scholarship in archaeology, anthropology, and demography reveals that both single women and married couples throughout the Western world relied on infant homicide as a routine method of family planning.[13] Ancient Greek and Roman law granted fathers the right to decide which offspring would be nurtured and raised and which would be killed or abandoned. While many in these societies exposed infants (leaving them outside for enough time to kill them) out of economic necessity or to eliminate those who appeared disabled, members of the elite in particular did so to avoid dividing their property, out of preference for a different sex, or, as the law explicitly encouraged, simply because they did not desire additional offspring.

Exposure of newborns was so widely practiced as to have profoundly influenced the structures of ancient societies—as historian Erkki Koskenniemi writes, "The life of an unwanted newborn was cheap indeed in ancient times."[14] The same is true for the early modern era as well. In Parma between 1609 and 1637, for example, married couples used infanticide as a means of controlling both family size and offspring sex. The historian Laura Hynes tracked parish registries and family status in the area against economic and military crises and windfalls, revealing that rural agricultural families displayed a preference for male offspring, whereas urban residents preferred females who could find paid labor in the vibrant textile industry or in other artisanal family businesses. The number of missing babies is shockingly large. Over the course of a mere twenty-eight years, the data reveals a shortage of between 300 and 400 female babies in rural communities and between 1,100 and 1,600 male infants in urban areas.[15]

In the early modern era, infant homicides took many forms. After exposure—which could lead to fortuitous family adoption, slavery, prostitution, death by hypothermia, dehydration, starvation, or being eaten by predators, depending on location and luck—most couples either underfed their infants to death over the course of a few days or induced suffocation by co-sleeping too closely. Fewer administered poison, stabbed their infants with thin, sharp objects, or stuffed their mouths and nostrils with fabric or dirt. Early forms of birth control and abortion were available to some but were not reliable, safe, or private, nor were they permissible according to religious doctrine. Accessing these methods of family planning would have required the mother to consciously recognize and then publicly admit to choosing to end her pregnancy. In contrast, passive or semi-voluntary methods of infanticide could remain a private, secret affair—even the mother herself would not have to view her actions as intentional or immoral. In the absence of pregnancy tests and with the prevalence of gastrointestinal diseases, it is likely that many pregnancies went undetected until after women could avail themselves of other strategies to limit the size of their families. And given that wolves, boars, and wild dogs were known to ravage live abandoned newborns, leaving their bloodied body parts in plain view, parents may well have considered an instant death at home to be an act of mercy.

Historians and anthropologists use a range of ambiguous terms to characterize the nature of these killings: infanticide could be an active, passive, or semi-voluntary act. In an early account of widespread anti-natalist practices, including both abortion and infant homicide, anthropologist Richard Trexler describes infanticide as both a specific goal and an "accidentally-on-purpose behavior" performed with unspoken community acceptance.[16] Infant and child mortality were also extremely common. Before 1760, as many as 40 percent of live-born infants passed prior to their seventh birthdays. As Hynes explains, "The high rates of infant mortality during most of the early modern period and the relatively low life expectancy brought death into every home and desensitized its occurrence."[17] For families with fewer resources, the arrival of a newborn could threaten the survival of an older toddler, who was likely still nursing. This specific survival competition among young children within families is likely part of why bonding between newborns and mothers does not occur instantaneously at birth, in contrast to most Hollywood portrayals of an infant's first moments, but actually deepens, both biologically and neurologically, over the first weeks of life.[18] In this murky social and psychological context, a mother who smothered or starved her newborn faced no compulsion to view herself unkindly. Given the prevalence of infant mortality, her community was unlikely to be suspicious or punish her in ways that would harm her older children.

Behavioral historian Gregory Hanlon has done more to uncover evidence of infanticide throughout Western history than any other, revealing both the prevalence of the practice and its coexistence with official censure. In *Death Control in the West 1500–1800*, Hanlon methodically analyzes 300 years of baptismal registers and ecclesiastical censuses from Catholic and Protestant communities across France, Italy, and England, demonstrating that infanticide was routinely practiced by married couples in Christian communities. He finds that families from all social strata—in good times and bad—practiced selective infanticide to manage resources and safeguard status, as was the case for populations across the globe before the advent of effective birth control and predictably safe abortion.

Prior to Hanlon, most historians misunderstood the rhetoric of elite males who condemned infant exposure in the texts that have survived long enough to be analyzed, interpreting their criticism of the practice as actual prohibition. Koskenniemi—an expert on infant exposure in ancient Greek and Roman civilizations and author of the most exhaustive analysis of both official religious texts and papyri, which capture more casual, interpersonal communications—concedes that early Jews and Christians practiced infant abandonment, but still concludes that official pronouncements against the practice must have restricted everyday behavior.[19]

Hanlon's research leapfrogs over the vacuum in historical documentation of Europeans' intimate family lives to reveal that official sanction and elite condemnation had no bearing on what parents did privately. Hanlon applies the tested research methods that have been used to study femicide in Eastern nations for decades—a process earlier scholars would have replicated, he says, if not for "the tenacious prejudice that Europeans behaved differently from other people throughout the globe"[20]—and finds that not only did married couples, many with older children, enact selective infanticide in a routine manner, but that these killings were also regularly overlooked, both publicly and privately. "Married mothers had no need to hide their pregnancy," Hanlon explains, because "authorities would have been reluctant to be too curious, for punishing the mother would have imperiled the lives of innocent toddlers."[21] A starved infant may have always appeared unable to thrive, a weakling; one that died more suddenly may have been stricken by any number of maladies known to afflict newborns. The innate vulnerability of new life allowed those who killed newborns to tell themselves and any witnesses that nature was the sole perpetrator.

Rhetoric at the time that condemned infant exposure focused on harm caused to the state, not the child, and would not have reached or influenced most of those who practiced it. Criticism of infant exposure and homicide from Christian theologians, then a religious minority, was used to mark their elevated ethical status. The myth that Christian parents refrained from infanticide, abortion, and other methods of restricting family size sustained the belief in Christian superiority, which in turn served as the ideological foundation for the Crusades and other colonialist projects that unleashed both actual infant homicide and infanticidal social and economic systems on an unrivaled global scale. By defining themselves in opposition to those who practiced selective infanticide, Christian theologians inadvertently created an enduring problem with punishment—evidence of infanticide within their community, which would give the lie to Christian superiority, demanded, and continues to demand, denial and a scapegoat to punish.

The intellectual history of infanticide in the West in turn rests on these false narratives. In but one prominent example of this ideology, John Brodhead Beck, a doctor and author of the first significant American study of infanticide in 1817, wrote that infanticide's "existence might have been supposed possible in those unhappy regions of our earth, where untutored passions and brutal sense reign triumphant over reason and morality; but that the fairest portions of society, where genius, science, and refinement had taken their abode, should have been disgraced by a crime so disgusting, is one of those anomalies in the history of human feeling and conduct, which irresistibly prove how perfectly arbitrary and undefined are the laws of justice and humanity, when unguided by the principles of true religion."[22] Even though Beck was well versed in the expansive history of infant homicide globally, his prejudice prompted him to view its occurrence in Upstate New York, where he was living when he wrote the statement above, as an aberration.

For eighteenth- and nineteenth-century Americans, infant abandonment, homicide, and mortality were all visible facts of life—absent from textbooks on the history of the United States today but present in court records, broadsides, ballads, and sermons from the colonial era forward that document infanticide prosecutions and executions. American literature of the time is replete with stories in which infant abandonment and homicide drive the plot. In nineteenth-century Chicago, historian Jeffrey Adler notes, urban dwellers found "dead infants in alleys and gutters, in trash heaps and privies, along desolate roads, and in any body of water" and "sewer workers, street cleaners, and policemen routinely found dead babies." While funerals and formal burials would be arranged for older children, newborns "with whom the bonding process was at best incomplete [were] not necessarily treated as members of the family or even human beings." Of these dead infants, Adler says, "Most probably died from natural causes."[23] Adler's use of the word "probably" is telling. Given many women's precarious social and financial status and the threat an additional child posed to the well-being of older toddlers, future marital opportunities, housing, and employment, infanticide could have been a survival strategy for many. As in earlier historical periods, seeking out birth control and abortion required an awareness of the pregnancy, extra income to cover the cost, an explicit intention to transgress ethical standards, and a willingness to accept potential health risks. Infanticide, by contrast, could be conducted privately, for free, and seemingly without intention, although with serious medical risk. Mothers' deaths while giving birth were common.

The prevalence of infant death in early American life presented a challenge both to the nascent criminal justice system and to increasingly sensitive, reform-oriented elite sensibilities. Leading up to and after the revolution, republican ideals vested motherhood with a new national significance, and mothers with the responsibility of raising a virtuous citizenry. These lofty principles elevated the status of mothering while also reinforcing women's place in the private, domestic sphere of the home, thereby excluding working women.[24] The visible presence of abandoned and dead babies raised troubling questions about the ability of American mothers to live up to these standards.

In this confusing context, male doctors saw an opportunity and a hazard. By the mid-eighteenth century, an ambitious new science in Europe and the United States, called both "medical jurisprudence" and "state medicine," sought to apply empirically vetted truths during court proceedings, particularly in cases involving poison, insanity, and infant homicide. The field was particularly concerned with the prevalence of infanticide and the struggle of coroners, appointed officials laboring with minimal compensation and even less training, to distinguish accidental and natural infant deaths from intentional murders. Women in marginal social and financial positions faced considerable legal risk when their babies' deaths were viewed as suspect and could be given the death penalty even in tragic circumstances where they had played little active role in the demise of their newborns—such as a stillbirth after an unattended labor or an inability to nurse a newborn immediately postpartum due to malnourishment and unrelenting work demands.

In these tragic and often unjust circumstances, doctors like Beck positioned themselves in early medical journals as saviors of female virtue laboring in service of the new republic's highest ideals. Beck and his peers insisted that their research on infant homicide would protect female vulnerability while enabling a more precise application of justice. Portraying themselves as neutral experts, they nevertheless transcribed bias into the fledgling legal practice and sought to elevate their own, often inaccurate, forensic observations above women's and working-class men's personal testimony during jury deliberations. The emergence of science did little to overcome the sentiments and stereotypes that continue to drive biased, incoherent policy and law governing infanticide.

Today, problems persist at the intersection of law and science. This tension is difficult to resolve, in part, because data collection on neonaticide and infant abandonment remains inadequate. No federal agency systematically tracks the number of infant homicides committed in the first twenty-four hours of life, technically termed "neonaticides," or the outcome of these cases in the criminal justice system. Anecdotal evidence from those working on the front lines of this issue, including emergency room (ER) nurses, coroners, and forensic psychiatrists, suggests that many girls and women suspected of committing infant homicide, today as in the past, are not viewed as criminals. Authorities routinely extend sympathy to cases ranging from high-achieving, middle- and upper-class, perfectionist high school students clinging desperately to a "good girl" self-image to impoverished child victims of the most severe domestic abuse and incest.

Beyond these ambiguous cases, which either solicit law enforcement's sympathy or are too medically murky to warrant prosecution, infanticide is also one of the only forms of homicide dogged by a significant "dark figure." Dark figure is a foundational concept in critical criminology. Coined to describe the limits of official crime statistics, it refers to the percentage of any type of crime that evades detection. It marks the difference between the crime rates reported by the state and the true but incalculable rates. Underage drinking and texting while driving are obvious examples of crimes with large dark figures. In contrast, most instances of homicide committed against adults and older children are investigated and prosecuted. Victims who are killed at birth, however, lack social ties: they are unknown, undocumented. Their corpses are easily concealed by technology as basic as a garbage bag or backpack. Infanticide's inevitable dark figure means that any attempt at quantification will be limited.

Yet, even when data can be successfully and comprehensively gathered, there is little indication of the political will to do so. No state or federal agency tracks the number of babies abandoned in hospitals in their first few days of life, despite the systematic documentation of these cases in medical insurance records. Unplanned, in-hospital infant abandonment is the modern-day equivalent of exposure, but in a location more likely to lead to adoption than discovery by wolves. Doctors and nurses on the front lines are alarmed by the increasing number of women in labor arriving at emergency departments having received no prenatal care, with no parenting plan, and grappling, along with their families, with a myriad of life crises, including addiction, poverty, and domestic abuse. As the director of the National Safe Haven Alliance and former ER nurse Heather Burner explains, those who call her hotline tend to be in crisis prior to becoming pregnant.[25]

Yet the last time the federal government tracked in-hospital abandonments was in the 1990s. By the late 1980s, with the crack epidemic underway as both a moral panic and a medical crisis, newspaper headlines condemned so-called crack moms, coded as Black, who were leaving infants in hospitals, claiming that the country was enduring an expensive "boarder baby" problem. Boarder baby was the term used at the time to describe newborn infants whose parents were either unwilling or unable to provide care and who ended up stuck in hospitals awaiting adoption or foster care placement after birth. Motivated to better understand the scope and scale of the boarder baby problem, lawmakers passed the Abandoned Infant Assistance Act in 1988, which allocated funds for the Department of Health and Human Services (HHS) to produce an annual estimate of the number of infants residing in hospitals despite being medically ready for discharge. Initially, HHS documented a concentration of in-hospital abandonments of drug-exposed infants in urban centers. A *Washington Post* article published in 1993, estimated that 22,000 babies had been abandoned in hospitals that year at an approximate cost of between $22 and $125 million.[26] Over time, however, the HHS observed a shift in demographics away from urban centers toward more rural areas and, even as numbers of abandoned infants appeared to be rising, political support for national reporting evaporated. The final report published in 1998, surveyed 926 hospitals in 113 jurisdictions, counting 17,400 in-hospital abandonments.[27] Despite today's ongoing opioid epic, however, no federal agency has monitored or reported on infant abandonment since 1998.

It is easy, as a researcher, to feel discouraged by the lack of adequate data and to worry about the harm wrought by misrepresentation. My research reveals that the legal and cultural history of infanticide in the United States has been defined by sexist stereotypes that continue to circulate, almost unchallenged. Yet we have arrived at a uniquely promising moment to turn the page. Over the course of the twentieth century and into the twenty-first, medical jurisprudence was overtaken by forensic psychiatry and interdisciplinary inquiry.[28] The offices of the coroner and medical examiner were reinvented as arms of law enforcement. After World War I, the discipline of forensic psychiatry gained public recognition as its practitioners demonstrated successful rehabilitation of veterans afflicted by war trauma or "shell shock." Often serving an evaluative function for court clinics and an expert witness role during infanticide trials, forensic psychiatrists today work at the intersection of medical knowledge and legal practice that Beck and his contemporaries attempted to claim.

The rise of forensic psychiatry, followed by successive waves of interdisciplinary research, facilitated new ways of understanding maternal violence that are just now coming to fruition. These major intellectual realignments shifted the focus from strictly medical observations of infants' corpses toward a deeper understanding of perpetrators' psyches and circumstances. Long-standing theories from forensic psychiatry now coexist with novel insights by historians, legal and cultural studies scholars, nurse practitioners, neuroscientists, and doctors. Putting these time-tested conclusions and new voices in conversation reveals that while contemporary cases of infanticide are widely viewed as unimaginable aberrations, they instead point to how humans have learned to cope with crisis and navigate punishingly competitive material and social hierarchies.

Popular accounts of infant homicide tend to zoom in on the psyche and morality of individual mothers. Yet, as this book demonstrates, these tragedies are socially and culturally situated in ways that require a wider, more nuanced analytic lens. Over the past fifty years, the study of infanticide has advanced from defining categories of culpability, an intellectual project not unlike profiling that requires generalization and abstraction, into an emerging sense of the heterogeneity of these cases, which instead demands greater individual specificity. This book's narrative case study approach is designed to contribute to critical scholarship that centers the complex personhood of those who commit acts of violence against family members.[29] This approach, best articulated by intra-family violence expert Neil Websdale, both situates individual perpetrators within interdependent social networks and attends to socially and culturally situated meanings.

Departing from mainstream psychology, Websdale argues that the "search for standardized information" used to generate categories and discern patterns across groups of perpetrators "ought *accompany* rather than eclipse the acquisition of personal, highly complex idiosyncrasies" (emphasis added).[30] In a practical sense this means shifting the focus away from profiling and prevention, which, I argue, previous research has overemphasized preemptively given the limits on what is known and what is knowable. Instead this book presents as neutral an observation of one tragedy's subtle interpersonal and emotional intricacies as possible.

In the chapters that follow, I trace how a wide range of actors, including coroners, prosecutors, judges, journalists, scientists, and community members living in proximity to these tragedies, have all helped shape the history of infant homicide in the United States in ways that continue to define the treatment of contemporary cases. Part I offers a detailed account of the two most significant episodes in the intellectual and legal history of American infanticide. Chapter 1 considers state medicine and Dr. John Brodhead Beck in the context of how infanticide cases were punished during the eighteenth and nineteenth centuries. Chapter 2 follows two overlapping twentieth- and twenty-first-century intellectual projects: one, the rise of forensic psychiatry in the late 1960s and Dr. Phillip J. Resnick's framework for understanding mothers who kill their own children, and two, the feminist legal studies and interdisciplinary research spearheaded by law professor Michelle Oberman, which shifted the focus from women's characteristics to their contexts and circumstances.

In Part II, I focus on Emile and Addison's case as an important contemporary example of the kind of infant homicide that receives the lion's share of public attention: neonaticides committed by young mothers and with salacious elements. Through an in-depth narrative case study of Emile and Addison, I document how the history and the popular mythology around infanticide detailed in Part I blow back on society's most vulnerable mothers and babies. I draw on in-depth life history interviews, videotaped interrogations and other police records, participant observations of legal proceedings, private correspondence, and social media posts—all to show how one infant death is a slow-moving crisis that takes place in plain view of the victim's community.

Ultimately, the book argues that the social, cultural, and evolutionary basis behind infant homicide is key to understanding contemporary tragedies, like Emile's, because these contexts reveal that the risk of committing infanticide is not cordoned off to a specific, identifiable group of deviant or damaged individuals who are distinct from everyone else.[31] There is no "other" to shun. Instead, all parents are potentially at risk of killing their offspring—under the worst circumstances and with the least support. The real mothers and fathers involved in these cases differ from each other and from the monster mom stereotype in dramatic ways. This book details historical and contemporary stories that illustrate the varied lives of those who commit infant homicide and the wildly different consequences they confront, from the death penalty to treatment to invisibility. This diversity underscores that the risk of infant homicide is more widespread than many recognize and therefore that efforts to prevent it need to be multifaceted, evidence-based, and well-resourced.

PART I

The Intellectual and Legal History of Infanticide

Science is a product of society. . . . That scientists might be unaware of the implications of their work does not make them any less mediators or marketeers of political ideas; for many this is a studied innocence. . . . Scientists need to become aware not just of how history shapes the present, but also how what is studied—and what has been neglected—grows out of who is doing the studying, and for what ends.

—*Londa Schiebinger,* Nature's Body: Gender in the Making of Modern Science

CHAPTER 1

"Innocent and Seduced" versus "Lewd and Cunning"

THE INVENTION OF BLAMELESS AND BLAMEWORTHY INFANTICIDAL MOTHERS

From late summer into early fall of 1821 in New York's Hudson Valley, Dr. John Brodhead Beck, a highly regarded expert on infanticide, kept hourly watch over the decomposing thoracic viscera of a stillborn infant. A mere twenty-four hours after a "very difficult and protracted labor," a doctor friend brought the infant's organs to Beck's estate and laboratory.[1] There is no record of whether the mother perished during her travail, leaving the infant's remains without a guardian, or if, so bereft, she volunteered the body to science. Her name is unknown. Her wishes for herself and her baby are lost to the historical record. Beck's detailed notes on the examination, however, are safely archived.

Almost 200 years later, Emile Weaver, like many other women prosecuted for neonaticide, would be charged with criminal abuse of a corpse for her efforts to clean up after a medically perilous, solitary labor. Ironically, these laws were originally enacted to rein in rampant grave robbery and secretive autopsies committed by doctors and medical students, like Beck. Yet no accusations of criminality were levied against Beck's friend, for theft of the infant corpse, or Beck, for further dismemberment of the body. Certainly, no disciplinary action was taken against them. It would have been antithetical to Beck's worldview to see his actions and those of his peers—all eager to advance their scientific understanding and solidify their professional stature—as anything other than the elevated enactment of the most noble, civic-minded ideals and religious virtues.

As Beck explained in his address to the "gentleman graduates" of New York's College of Physicians and Surgeons, they were "not merely . . . recipients of professional knowledge, but also moral agents, destined to exert a wide influence, either for good or evil, on those around" them.[2] Beck's dearest hope was that as these graduates became "busy actors in the drama of human life," they would work toward "elevating and improving the profession . . . and bless society with their virtues."[3] Grave robbery and corpse defilement were but necessary means of accessing the scientific material needed to teach anatomy and advance medical research.[4]

Upon receiving the stillborn infant's organs, Beck prepared to repeat a forensic procedure called the hydrostatic, or more colloquially "floating lung," test, which had been developed by German and French doctors to assist with infanticide prosecutions where it was uncertain if an infant had been born alive, long enough to breathe, or stillborn. Before starting the test, Beck placed the baby's heart, lungs, and thymus gland in a basin of water and observed that they readily sank to the bottom and that "no symptoms of putrefaction were discernable." Three days after the baby's birth, Beck filled "vessels convenient and capacious" with "pure rain water," then immersed one intact lung and one lung cut into smaller sections. Both lobes sank to the bottom of the basin. He then exposed the lungs to "the rays of an intense sun," starting the process of decomposition.[5]

Five hours later, Beck observed that the lungs had begun to float, air bubbles were now visible on their surfaces, and the basins had begun to emit a "very offensive" odor. Beck continued to track the movements of the lungs multiple times daily, carefully refilling the basins with rainwater as needed. Eleven days later, the lungs had permanently settled to the bottom of the vessel and "never afterwards showed any disposition to float, although suffered to stand for better than five weeks."[6]

To Beck, the lungs had behaved predictably. "In the incipient stage of putrefaction," he wrote, "lungs that have never respired will float in water; whereas they will sink, if it has continued long enough to completely destroy their organization, and thus extricate all the air contained in them." Beck clarifies that his results have been corroborated by numerous other hydrostatic tests, and that the test's validity is clear given that "a case perfectly analogous is witnessed in every person that is drowned."[7]

Despite his stated confidence in the test, however, Beck repeated it many times throughout his career to disprove the test's many critics and to support its frequent use in infanticide trials. Beck conducted the specific test described here as further evidence to support this argument for a medical journal article. Beck's chief cause was justice for infants and fetuses, both groups he championed throughout his career and whose healthcare he labored to improve through research into infant therapeutics. For Beck and his contemporaries, the term "infanticide" included both infant homicide and abortion.[8] Beck was also nothing if not rigorous. His contemporaries applauded his *Inaugural Dissertation on Infanticide* as "the standard work" on the topic and one that had "completely exhausted the subject."[9] The book included in-depth reviews of travelogues documenting abortion and infanticide everywhere from Iceland to Fiji and referenced hundreds of experiments, including several that aimed to discern the difference between fetal and newborn infant blood by dissecting fetal guinea pigs and puppies "while yet in the womb of their mother."[10] The central question of medical jurisprudence, he wrote, was differentiating a naturally occurring infant death from an intentional infant homicide, using the physical remains of the deceased newborn alone.[11] The hydrostatic test, Beck argued, could be relied upon to demonstrate if an infant had been born alive enough to breathe, and therefore whether it had been deliberately killed.

From the vantage point of the twenty-first century, it is hard to fathom the centrality of infanticide in American life in the 1800s. For Beck and his circle, however, the need to reliably distinguish between naturally occurring stillbirth and other incidents of infant mortality, accidental infant death, and intentional infant homicide committed in stealth by unwed mothers—without resorting to the advice of midwives or the gossip of the mothers' community members, whom Beck describes as "old wives and quacks"—was a matter of pressing importance and frequent professional embarrassment.[12] They focused on "unwed mothers" because regulations adopted by the colonies from British common law singled out "lewd women that have been delivered of bastard children" for prosecution, turning a blind eye to similar actions by married women—though a different statute allowed for prosecution of married women and men for murders committed against older children. Fourteen child homicide cases were prosecuted in the Massachusetts Bay Colony between 1630 and 1696, and many similar cases, historian Dustin Griffin writes, "no doubt . . . escaped legal notice."[13]

Medicine, as Beck and his contemporaries practiced it, was just as likely to inflict suffering as mitigate it; many patients at the time opted instead for homeopathic remedies or midwives' services. The very first American medical schools were just starting to define their curriculums and issue degrees. The men whom these schools accredited came from close-knit, elite families and were just beginning to advocate for public recognition of their questionably useful skillset.

Beck and his older brother, Theodric Romeyn (1791–1855), also an internationally renowned expert in state medicine, were born into this circle of influence. Their maternal grandfather founded Union College. Their uncle, who supervised John Beck's early education, was the pastor of the Reformed Church in Rhinebeck, New York. Later, when John Beck attended Columbia College, his uncle served as a trustee and introduced Beck to the provost, "who took great delight in encouraging and guiding his progress."[14] The Becks' father died when they were still young, which perhaps explains the surplus of paternal affection they received from other family members and friends. Both brothers went on to enjoy extensive professional success: John was elected to serve as a trustee of the College of Physicians and Surgeons; as a censor, vice president, and then president of the County Medical Society; and as vice president, then president of the State Medical Society. He cofounded *The New York Medical and Physical Journal*, edited it for seven years, and published many of his own articles in it. The brothers' coauthored volume *Elements of Medical Jurisprudence* (1823) was reprinted twelve times in the United States and four times in Britain and was translated into German and Swedish.

While the Becks enjoyed the respect of their professional peers on two continents, they were preoccupied with winning legitimacy for the increasingly professionalized American medical field—among patients generally but also specifically in legal settings, where doctors' testimony during criminal investigations and prosecutions, particularly infanticide cases, was often dismissed. In a February 6, 1828, address to the "Gentlemen of the Medical Society of the State of New York," Theodric Beck, then serving as the society's president, elaborated on his "anxious wish to elevate the character of our common profession."[15] Convinced that medical knowledge could improve the enactment of law, the Becks envisioned and advocated for dramatic changes to American coroners' offices based on practices in Germany and France—changes that would not come to pass until after their deaths.

In the early republic, American coroners were called in when members of a community found a death suspicious. They were appointed to their positions and many lacked any kind of medical training or even basic anatomical instruction, so would often call on doctors for help, for little or no compensation, when a corpse required examination. Doctors' professional testimony in turn was often discredited publicly in ways that could damage their reputations and make securing paid work more difficult. They were also pitted against each other by dueling prosecutors and defense attorneys. Courts were right to be skeptical of their testimony, however; as historian James Mohr explains, "most American physicians were too poorly trained in systematic methods and forensic applications to be significantly useful in any event."[16] Theodric Beck himself admitted that a doctor could be a skilled practitioner "yet not be competent as a witness."[17]

During contentious infanticide trials, both Becks were highly critical of the legal system's tendency to rely on circumstantial evidence. Factors such as whether a woman concealed her pregnancy or prepared for the postpartum period were traditionally used to prove guilt or innocence. These kinds of considerations often made the difference between the accused being executed or exonerated. Reliance on such evidence was "without the least foundation in justice," insisted Beck. He argued that these unscientific legal norms inadvertently favored more experienced, "cunning" women, who would know how to thwart a jury. A more naive woman, by contrast, he explained, might conceal a pregnancy due to her "remaining spark of virtuous feeling" and fail to procure clothing and other supplies for the baby before its birth out of inexperience or fear of asking for help.[18]

As Beck's critique of relying on circumstantial evidence highlights, he focused relentlessly on ways to provide coroners with more reliable, valid sources of evidence, to make justice in infanticide cases a matter of neutral, empirical judgment. But his resistance to existing legal methods was not as impactful as he hoped; the same exact circumstantial considerations are still used by prosecutors today to sway jurors' impressions of guilt, as Emile's case demonstrates. And, perversely, in rejecting the validity of circumstantial evidence, Beck ended up reinforcing an equally unscientific set of sexist assumptions about different types of blameless and blameworthy infanticidal mothers that also continue to play an outsized role in legal practice and popular culture. As the rhetoric of "seduced" and "lewd" suggests, Beck presupposed certain innate, socially visible maternal characteristics could be relied upon to discern which infanticidal mothers were victims of men's desires, and thus worthy of sympathy and lenience, and which were instead "cunning," "lewd," and deserving of death.[19] His focus on forensics, seen from this angle, was designed to help identify cunning women while protecting their sympathetic counterparts. Wildly durable, these same sentimental categories of moral distinction—between hapless and conniving, between victim and slut, between loving and indifferent, between self-sacrificing and self-interested—continue to be the cornerstone of today's monster mom stereotype.

While there remains a great depth of evidence documenting doctors' views on infant homicide, the vast majority of actual historical infanticide cases are impossible to describe in any measure of meaningful detail. Due to the relative ease of concealing an infant's corpse, most infant homicides were never discovered and thus never reported. Even when dead infants were found, the absence of DNA testing made identifying a perpetrator impossible—unless those living in proximity to the crime chose to involve themselves. Historians rely primarily on coroners' inquest reports, jail logs, court documents, broadsides, newspapers, sermons, medical journals, the diaries of prominent male members of society, and, in cases where a high-profile attorney rendered service, his archived notes and correspondences. These kinds of sources shed light exclusively on cases where a suspect was identified, cases that came under official scrutiny, and cases that were deemed newsworthy—likely outliers, rather than typical or representative cases. There is also no way of determining whether the cases on the record were actual infant homicides or wrongful convictions. When women's names are recorded in these documents, they are often spelled differently by the coroner, the jailer, and the journalist, making accurate identification a dead end. Babies are barely mentioned in these accounts. They pass unnamed, their sex unspecified.

Statistics from Baltimore between 1835 and 1860 illustrate the problems with documentation of infant abandonment and homicide. At least 976 inquests were performed upon the discovery of a dead infant corpse during that time, but *The Baltimore Sun* reported on fewer than 300 of these tragedies. Twenty-nine women were indicted; thirteen show up on jail logs; six went to trial and were either acquitted or had their cases dismissed. The only known conviction for infant homicide during this time period was Gustavus Struth, a male German immigrant farmer, who beat his ten-month-old son to death while his wife was napping. Struth was charged with second-degree murder, not infanticide, and served nearly eighteen years in prison.[20] As these numbers suggest, newspapers and court documents present a limited image of infanticide. An unusual anthropological account of New York's Five Points neighborhood in the mid-nineteenth century analyzed the physical remains of two, likely twin, newborns and a fetus (gestational age estimated to be between twenty-two and twenty-four weeks) who were found stacked in a single privy next to a brothel.[21] These deaths, which could have been miscarriages, stillbirths, or an abortion and infanticide, would be invisible to a researcher working with the other sources listed above.

Whereas European historians have carefully documented infanticide on a national level, there has yet to be a systematic historical account of infanticide in the United States.[22] American historians have examined individual colonies, states, and cities during specific time periods, revealing some local factors conducive to infanticide or impacting the status of women in the area but not overarching trends in infanticide rates or prosecutions. These studies do demonstrate regional variations in rhetoric around and punishment of infanticide, however, suggesting that factors such as a community's stage of development (from frontier outpost to more established jurisdiction), and ethnic and religious demographics played a defining role in determining when an infanticide would be investigated and who would ultimately be punished for the crime.

In early Massachusetts, prominent infanticide cases triggered sermons on uncleanliness and parental authority delivered by the most prominent Puritan preachers, followed by public hangings on Boston Common. Similarly in Connecticut, public hangings of Indigenous servants and enslaved people, as young as twelve years old, for the crime of infanticide drew upward of 10,000 spectators who listened to the most esteemed, Harvard-educated ministers preach against lust, "sins against our own bodies," and insist on the virtues of maintaining the social hierarchy.[23] In the mid-Atlantic and further south, high-status men with property, often connected to plantations, presided over infanticide trials. Bedecked in expensive courtroom attire including tassels and medallions, they performatively reasserted their dominance over women whose transgressive behavior might undermine the shaky hierarchy but rarely followed through with conviction or punishment.[24]

Demographics seem likely to have played an important role in these significant regional variations. In southern jurisdictions where women were fewer in number, their social value may have limited their vulnerability to execution. On a local level, perhaps an invisible equation weighed the value of women to society against the value of punishing women who were deemed a threat to the patriarchal social order, with some women possessing greater social value than others based on factors such as race, nationality, family status, sexual propriety, and appearance.

Throughout the country, the quality of individual interpersonal relationships played a decisive role in who would be publicly accused and who would be granted privacy. Women and working-class men held sway during the first critical stage in infanticide investigations, before an accusation was made. Friends, neighbors, and housemates who may have observed a weight gain or noticed signs of a birth could choose to investigate and report or turn a blind eye. Midwives were called upon to confirm rumored pregnancies, assess potentially aborted or miscarried fetuses, and determine if dead neonates had been stillborn or murdered. If the infant's death was deemed sufficiently suspicious, an initial inquest jury was formed. This investigative body was usually comprised of men from the suspect's immediate community, who often found reasons to forgo further prosecution. Inquest juries frequently condemned mothers for being neglectful but softened their assessment by adding that natural causes were ultimately to blame. Occasionally an infant's death was even explained as a "visitation of God."[25]

These community-level, intimate, interpersonal factors led to significant discrepancies between even neighboring jurisdictions in frequency of investigation, conviction, and punishment. In Pennsylvania, Lancaster and Dauphin counties alone generated 35 percent of all infanticide convictions and most of the state's executions before 1800. Even more dramatically, in Baltimore, the "quirks of a single coroner" led to a threefold increase in infanticide investigations in 1857. In reaction to this unprecedented spike, Maryland officials "expressed annoyance that coroners were investigating more deaths than were strictly necessary out of a desire to use their office for personal gain: coroners were paid by the case."[26]

Most local studies on the subject suffer from the same gap in historical data: the experiences and perceptions of prosecuted women and their babies prior to, during, and after their trials. The women whose stories have been preserved on the historical record did not write diaries or deathbed confessions or, if they did, these texts were not archived. Instead, we are left with documents published and preserved by members of society with higher status and more education than the accused, such as sermons and diaries written by prominent preachers, other formal legal documents, and journalism. Historians eager to determine infanticidal women's motives do so at the risk of mistaking public perceptions and imposed stereotypes for women's actual desires for themselves and their offspring during experiences that were fundamentally medical ordeals. Severe medical trauma experienced in isolation does not lend itself naturally to coherent narratives. Memory works to erase and rewrite experiences of this dreadful variety. Some of the women in cases like these may not even have seen themselves as taking action, or may simply have experienced a stillbirth. When we find coherent stories on the record, we should be suspicious as to their origin; historians' conclusions can draw only from the legal and cultural processes that adjudicated and reported on a select few cases and reflect political agendas, sentiments, and stereotypes from the time.

Women from all class backgrounds exercised power when they accused their neighbors of infanticide and participated in investigations and prosecutions. Given that individual intimate relationships were the single most significant determining factor in whether a suspicious infant death was recorded, it is devastating from a research perspective to have no evidence that can shed light on why women chose to report other women in some cases and helped with concealment in others. There are cases on the record where a woman's mother reported her, but no explanation for why, and still other cases where family members, spouses, and coworkers chose to be complicit in concealment. Still others faced with evidence of infanticide in their community endeavored to protect the moral order. Some reporting may have been driven by religious conviction or ethical outrage or designed to distance the reporter from the stigma carried by the to-be-accused. Many of these tragedies occurred in tight living quarters shared by domestic servants where hidden social economies of reliance and resentment may have been in play.

Women on the other side of the equation, who committed various forms of infant homicide undetected, found agency in evasion, in their ability to slip below the radar and escape investigation. Their absence from the historical record is the only trace of control they exerted over their constrained circumstances. For women who found themselves accused of infanticide, it is unclear what, if any, control they exercised over how their actions were made sense of in the public sphere. Even their confessions were likely written by men. Diaries of prominent ministers in Massachusetts and Connecticut reveal how these spiritual leaders sought to influence women convicted of infanticide ahead of their executions, exerting pressure on them to confess from the gallows using language scripted for them by the ministers that served these men's agendas. When women were too petrified or tearful to speak with the noose around their neck, these statements were read for them.[27] Acting as ventriloquists for the moral order, these statements play into the same set of myths and stereotypes Beck suggested could be relied upon to distinguish the innocent from the guilty. Perhaps some women came to see themselves in these familiar narratives or leaned on these dominant cultural scripts to make sense of their actions in the most sympathetic light possible.

Rather than attempting to discern motives in these records, however, it is far more historically sound to trace how infanticide cases became flashpoints for local and national political debates over everything from the enforcement of religious norms, to sexual propriety, to the status of women and babies in society, to slavery and abolition. The few infanticide cases for which in-depth historical records survive demonstrate the missteps doctors at the time made as legal witnesses and the misconceptions they shared with lawyers, preachers, and the press about the causes of infanticide. Doctors like Beck, male family members with status, lawyers, prosecutors, the press, midwives, and friends and family of the accused who were called to testify invented a set of motives rife with sexist assumptions about women's behavior to explain infanticidal actions, in ways that both sanitized and sensationalized them.

With an awareness of the limitations on what is known and what is knowable, we can consider the versions of the stories left on the historical record of Elizabeth Emerson, Alice Clifton, Hannah Jenkins, and Margaret Garner. These cases stand out because each woman's personal traumas became rhetorical opportunities for other, more prominent members of society to advance their own religious and political viewpoints. There is therefore a surplus of speech to analyze related to these cases.

Elizabeth Emerson's case is one of the earliest well-documented American infanticides. Her conviction unfolded well before John Beck's lifetime and helps demonstrate why Beck and his peers took issue with how infanticides were prosecuted when medical expert's insights were not respected over other forms of testimony. The night of May 8, 1691, twenty-six-year-old Elizabeth labored in silence on a trundle at the foot of her sleeping parents' bed. Her consistent testimony, given multiple times under pressure, was that the twin girls she delivered were born dead; that she concealed her pregnancy and declined to call for help while in labor because she was afraid that it would kill her mother to wake up and discover the situation; that after the labor, she placed the dead twins in a truck; and that two days later, when her parents were out of the house at a weekly church service, she sewed them into a linen sack and attempted to bury them in the backyard. Her parents, also under repeated and intense interrogation, insisted that they had heard nothing during the labor, and had no awareness of it or their daughter's pregnancy.[28]

If Emerson's parents had confirmed her testimony and stated that they had seen the babies born dead, the inquiry against their daughter would have had no grounds to advance. They declined to offer such testimony and thus chose to protect themselves from legal risk. Fifteen years earlier, Emerson's father had been fined five shillings by Essex County Court "for his cruel and excessive beating" and "kicking" of Emerson.[29] Court documents say the beating was done "with a flayle swingle":[30] two long wooden rods connected by a short metal chain, used like a scythe. Historians have wondered if Emerson feared her parents more than the magistrate. Emerson also witnessed five of her nine siblings die in infancy, and she states in recorded testimony that she was primarily concerned with how her actions might impact her mother's will to live.

The twins were not Emerson's first pregnancy outside of marriage. On April 10, 1686, she gave birth to a daughter, Dorothie, who survived less than a year. It was not uncommon for residents of the Massachusetts Bay Colony, and even members of Emerson's own family, to shake off charges of fornication (a sin punishable by whipping or a fine, or both) by quickly marrying once the first signs of pregnancy surfaced. Yet Emerson failed to secure Dorothie's father's proposal—historian Dustin Griffin suggests that Emerson and her family might have been "unable to bring enough moral or legal pressure to bear on the family of the putative father."[31]

Five years later, Emerson was pregnant again, with twins. If Emerson's pregnancy had somehow eluded her kin with whom she resided, the rest of Haverhill, a frontier-like outpost of Boston at the time, took notice and gossip spread about her rising apron strings, her family's reputation likely worsening. Two days after the twins' birth, local magistrate Nathaniel Saltonstall sent a delegation of two men and four women to the Emerson home with a warrant to examine Emerson's body and search the property, notifying Emerson that it had been "commonly reported" that she was pregnant. They arrived less than half an hour after Emerson had finished burying the twins and while her parents were still at church, an indication that the magistrate was surveilling the property.

Three of the four female members of the delegation, who were experienced in midwifery and postpartum care, were familiar to Emerson. Judith Webster was the second wife of Emerson's uncle; Hannah Swan was likely a relative of the man Emerson had named as Dorothie's father; Mary Neff was a family friend who would assist Emerson's sister, Hannah Duston, six years later during her postpartum recovery. They performed a physical examination of Emerson and found the dead twins' shallow grave, reporting back to Saltonstall that Emerson had "been newly delivered of a child" and that they believed the twins had been born healthy and alive but died shortly after birth due to "want of help and care at the time of travail"—that Emerson had not provided or requested the care the twins needed after their delivery in order to survive. The female delegates declined to determine "whether it was a willful act of Murder by the Mother or any else."[32]

Saltonstall next impaneled a coroner's inquest jury, which included the women from the initial delegation, to examine the corpses of the twins and interview Emerson again. No one with the kind of forensic skills Beck advocated for and taught would have been available at that time in Massachusetts, meaning that no autopsy or hydrostatic test could have been performed to help reinforce or contradict the circumstantial evidence. The jurors found no "mark of blows, or signs of being violently put to death" on the twins. Emerson, still only two days postpartum, was too ill to appear in court. Instead, she was interrogated "as she lay upon her bed."[33]

During this interview, Emerson named the twins' father: Samuel Lad, a forty-year-old father of eight children, six living at the time of the inquest, also from Haverhill, with a wife of fourteen years who was four months pregnant with their ninth child. Emerson stated, and others confirmed, that she met Lad regularly at an inn and that they had been together, and been seen together, the evening before the birth. Aside from Emerson's testimony, Lad appears nowhere else in the court's records. He was not prosecuted for fornication.

Five days after Emerson's labor, Saltonstall charged her with "whore-dome," for fornication and adultery, and took her into custody under "vehement suspicion of murder" for having concealed the labor and birth and the twins' bodies.[34] It took Saltonstall an additional four months to charge Emerson with infanticide. The delay in the murder charge likely had more to do with the law itself as opposed to the circumstantial nature of the evidence against Emerson. After five years of legislative debate, much of which occurred while Emerson's case was in the public eye, the Massachusetts Bay Colony formally incorporated Britain's 1624 infanticide statute (21 James 1, c. 27) into its legal code. Historian Dustin Griffin argues that the preamble to the statute, which soon spread to criminal codes throughout the colonies, "almost sounds like it was written with the Emerson case in mind":

> Whereas, many lewd women that have been delivered of bastard children, to avoid their shame, and to escape punishment, do secretly bury or conceal the death of their children, and after, if the child be found dead, the said woman do allege, that the said child was born dead; whereas it falleth out sometimes (although hardly it is to be proved) that the said child or children were murthered by the said women, their lewd mothers, or by their assessment or procurement . . . in every such case the said mother so offending shall suffer death as in case of murther . . . except such mother can make proof by one witness at the least, that the child (whose death was by her so intended to be concealed) was born dead.[35]

The statute made the act of concealing a pregnancy sufficient grounds for an infanticide conviction, which entailed a death sentence, but it also offered relief for any accused woman who could rally even one witness to testify that her infant was born dead. So harsh that it undermined jurors' willingness to convict, making consistent, fair punishment impossible, the statute was infamous for frustrating prosecutors in both Britain and the colonies. Pennsylvania was the first state to revise the statute, shifting the burden of proof onto prosecutors in 1776 and giving prosecutors and jurors a wider range of potential charges to consider, all of which entailed lesser sentences, in 1793.

Griffin makes an important point that the version of Emerson "accessible to us in court records" is "in effect constructed by the 1624 statute." "What we know of her depends on the questions asked of her and of the other witnesses," Griffin explains, "and those questions were designed to determine whether she fit the profile of the 'lewd women' of the statute."[36] This method of questioning appears in records from the same period of other particularly harsh prosecutions of single women for infanticide. Of the ten other cases brought to conviction in Massachusetts during the 1690s, only one woman was acquitted and spared death.

Emerson was charged with infanticide by the equivalent of a modern-day grand jury. The jury asserted that she had delivered two "live bastard" children and had murdered and buried them under "the Instigation of the Divil (original spelling)."[37] Without any evidence beyond what the delegation had gathered initially, the jurors brought forward a charge of intentional, premeditated infanticide against Emerson. At this stage in the prosecution, Emerson may well have found greater leniency from the court if she had changed her plea to guilty and played up her helplessness in the face of male seduction. She held to her original testimony, however, and continued to assert that while she had concealed her pregnancy and secretly buried the twins because she feared her parents' reaction, the babies had been born dead. She expressed remorse for disobeying her parents, less for the affair, none for the infants' stillbirth. There is no way, in retrospect, to assess the accuracy of Emerson's self-defense. It is worth lingering over where she drew the line, however. Emerson was willing to sacrifice her life and defy religious leaders to steadfastly reject the accusation that she had harmed her living babies. She was unwilling to participate in allowing herself to be defined as a callous, selfish mother.

In contrast to the delay leading up to the indictment, Emerson's trial started the day she was charged. Emerson could have vetted and rejected members of the jury but declined to do so.[38] Instead of live testimony, witnesses' statements were read in open court. Emerson defended herself, but her remarks were not recorded. She was found guilty of premeditated infanticide and sentenced to death by hanging, though the execution was delayed three years while the witchcraft trials proceeded—trials in which Emerson's cousin, Martha Toothaker Emerson, was examined but not prosecuted.

Cotton Mather, the prominent Harvard-educated Puritan preacher, visited Emerson while she was in prison and tried to persuade her to include expressions of guilt and remorse in the speech she would deliver at her execution. On April 25, 1693, the day of Emerson's hanging, Mather preached the execution sermon before a large crowd he described as "one of the greatest assemblies, ever known in these parts of the world."[39] Reflecting back on the significant occasion, he noted in his diary that he had long awaited an opportunity to preach from Job 36:14 on the "sins of uncleanliness," but fretted that despite his best efforts, Emerson had not admitted to killing her twins in an intentional, premeditated manner in her final speech.[40] Her lack of appropriate remorse did not prevent Mather from publishing her story and dying speech on several occasions as a cautionary tale. His attention to Emerson's case and writings on it, both personal and public, are the main reasons her case is known today.

To make a "more impressive moral lesson," Emerson was hanged on Boston Common at the same time as a "young black woman," also convicted of infanticide whose final speech from the gallows, if one exists, was not recorded.[41]

One piece of evidence exists that Emerson was not universally condemned. Emerson's older sister, Hannah Duston, became a well-known, if controversial, heroine. On March 15, 1697, Duston was captured in a raid by Abénaki natives from her home in Haverhill. Her infant was thrown against a tree during the raid and died. Three weeks after her capture, Hannah and two others who had also been taken in the raid returned to Haverhill with the scalps of ten Indigenous family members, which they sought to redeem for payment from the colony. The law allowed colonists to kill Indigenous people in self-defense, but Hannah had strategically and intentionally returned, after escaping to safety, to attack the family. Cotton Mather celebrated and retold Hannah's story, but she declined his requests to interview her. Later literary accounts by John Whittier, Nathaniel Hawthorne, and Henry Thoreau retell Hannah's story as "a dark and ambiguous tale of the passions and violence of old New England."[42] Hannah named her second daughter after her younger sister, Elizabeth.

For gentlemen like Beck and other advocates of state medicine, the application of justice in Emerson's case was no better than a medieval popularity contest. In the absence of any forensic investigation of the twins' corpses or hydrostatic test, jurors had only the accounts of midwives and other circumstantial considerations to help them arrive at their judgment. Cases like Emerson's exemplified the legal status quo that Beck and his peers labored unsuccessfully to improve.

In Pennsylvania in 1787, over 100 years after Emerson's hanging, the investigation and prosecution of a young Black woman named Alice Clifton reveals that the legal system continued to rely on the same circumstantial concerns, sentiments, and stereotypes. Little had improved in terms of the quality of the state's investigative apparatus. Historian G. S. Rowe explains that inquests at the time were, in general, "amateur" and that in Clifton's case the coroner was "careless." Rowe describes the chaotic, unprofessional nature of the investigation into Clifton's infant's death: "Besides failing to make and maintain a 'written examination' of Clifton and members of the household in which she lived because he [the coroner] 'did not know it was necessary,' he permitted the defendant to be interrogated by numerous people when, because the room was 'so crowded,' he could not 'clearly hear' her responses. It was only after the coroner had examined the child and talked with the mother (as had several members of the family and inquest jury) that it was discovered that the child's throat had been cut from ear to ear."[43] Confusion surrounded the physical evidence in her case; in addition to the coroner's missteps, the two doctors who had been called upon to examine the infant's corpse admitted under cross-examination at the trial that they had made an initial determination based on reports from the defendant and several members of the coroner's inquest jury, rather than examining the baby themselves. This confusion prompted the attorney general to pivot to more traditional, nonscientific concerns with the social performance of selfless maternal affection. In the absence of forensic tests, prosecutors asked jurors to consider if Clifton had "the benefit of linens"—whether she had prepared for the baby's arrival by making clothing and other blankets—and her emotional reaction to the infant's death. The attorney general "took considerable pains to have witnesses offer a judgment whether Miss Clifton cried, and if so, whether she wept over her own fate, or that of the dead child."[44]

Clifton claimed in her defense that she had been raped and that the baby was stillborn. She was represented by two of the state's top attorneys, both members of the abolitionist society, who "pounded away on the theme that all evidence suggested that the child was dead at birth, that if it had made a single sound, it would easily have been heard by people nearby." They described Clifton as helpless, uneducated, and submissive—convincing the judge, who characterized her in a manner that would have come across as sympathetic, as "a mute, slave, young illiterate, and ignorant."[45]

Despite her attorneys' efforts, however, the jury found Clifton guilty of infanticide under the state statute, modeled on Massachusetts' infanticide law. The conviction entailed an automatic death sentence, by hanging. As soon as the conviction was rendered, however, Clifton's attorneys appealed to the governor and secured a pardon—a reversal that highlights the contentious nature of infanticide cases, which could surface tensions between different segments of the population. Clifton's jury, appalled by the concrete evidence of violence done to the infant's corpse, found the governor's pardon a "perversion of authority by gentlemen."[46] Clifton's racial and class status likely made her actions more legible to elites who viewed maternal affection as the province of white women with means; Black women and poor women were assumed to be "unfeeling" mothers with latent criminality.[47] Only the most radical abolitionists applied the same language of natural maternal affection to enslaved women.

The governor's pity for Clifton is one example of a broader inclination to exonerate in infanticide trials that appears to have grown over the course of the eighteenth century.[48] Rowe observes growing "sympathy and compassion for the young women in infanticide proceedings" in Pennsylvania's court records from the time and increasingly rare convictions, noting that, of the twenty-two women charged with infanticide between 1768 and 1786 in Pennsylvania under the infanticide statute, including Clifton, only five were convicted. Of the five, only three convictions ended in executions. Two of the women hanged for infanticide were "mature women with histories of sexual deviation." The third was Black. And in all three cases, the infant's death had been "indisputably violent." These numbers and demographics suggest that the letter of the law was more rigid than actual legal norms except in cases where the accused was an outsider.[49]

In Maryland, historians have observed a similar bias driving the targeting of infanticide investigations and a similar inclination to exonerate all but the most marginalized, transgressive defendants. Historian Amanda Miracle finds that court documents from seventeenth-century colonial Maryland reveal a tendency to let wealthy defendants escape conviction. Katie M. Hemphill observes that the women who appear in Baltimore court documents from 1835 through 1860 were "socially marginalized because of their race or their lack of familiar connections with the city and they labored in ways that could be greatly hindered by pregnancy." But jurors were still inclined to let defendants off the hook, and "grasped for some evidence" in order to do so, in violation of the law.[50]

The case of Hannah Jenkins helps illustrate these colonial-era trends in Maryland, as well as the more subtle dynamics of female agency and power. In 1668, Jenkins was brought before the Kent County Court, accused of having delivered an illegitimate baby in secret, without assistance, and killed it to hide her transgression. Jenkins was the stepdaughter of George Harris, a well-known member of the local planter elite, who she lived with and who represented Jenkins during her initial court appearance, where he "spoke at length on her behalf." The jury, which was comprised of wives of elite men who presided over the court, listened to Jenkins's stepfather opine on her virtue and, confident that she was "a well-governed member of a strong patriarch's household," determined that she had never been pregnant in the first place. Jenkins was spared the kind of invasive physical exam that had been conducted on Emerson in the Massachusetts Bay Colony. No medical expert testified and no physical evidence of the birth was presented in court, as there appears to have been no investigation of Jenkins and Harris's residence. The justices of the court dismissed the charges against her.[51]

Jenkins's reliance on Harris to speak on her behalf suggests that she had the social and cultural savvy to "employ symbols of authority" to her advantage and thereby appear less threatening to the social order, which allowed the prosecution to relent—though she may simply have submitted to his authority because of social pressure to do so. "Those in power viewed the defendant in relation to her stepfather," Miracle argues, "and she in turn explicitly acknowledged the power dynamic that dictated her subordinate status and dependance on his goodwill. . . . He spoke for her and for all intents and purposes he ultimately controlled her."[52]

Public discourse on infanticide assumed that these tragedies occurred because women could not endure the shame wrought by male seduction and abandonment. The period's most popular literary works, including Susanna Rowson's bestselling *Charlotte Temple*, present highly sympathetic, sentimental versions of this tragic trope in which the seduced young woman inevitably dies because of her misfortune. She is the object of pity. These narratives evoke sympathy while also distracting from the harsh realities working-class women endured daily, including malnutrition, relentless employer demands, overcrowding, and loss of employment and housing as soon as they became visibly pregnant. In her review of nineteenth-century court documents and newspaper articles from Baltimore, Hemphill notes that while working-class women were not likely to share the same values and ideals as their employers, they could "craft narratives in which they were victims of malice rather than perpetrators of it" and thus exploit sexist stereotypes to win leniency.[53] In the absence of other financial and social assets, a woman's awareness of the stereotypes imposed upon her and willingness to embrace them could become legal capital—her degree of agency determined by her skill in harnessing these politics for self-defense. A woman could elicit sympathy by leaning into the stereotypes that were written into the law and inscribed in popular accounts, both fictional and journalistic—a strategy whose effectiveness likely varied based on her appearance, accent, attire, and other markers of status and identity. Alternatively, she could stay silent and hope that a man with rank would advocate on her behalf. Asserting her innocence proactively would have been a terribly ill-advised legal strategy.

The story behind Margaret Garner's failed prosecution further illustrates how high-profile infanticide trials have been used by social actors with more status than the accused as platforms for their own political agendas. Garner is the most well-known infanticidal figure from American history. The constitutional issues raised by her case forced a political conflict between the federal and Ohio state governments. National press outlets reported on Garner's case in serial installments, calling it an illustration of the "deep personal tragedy of slavery."[54] Numerous editorials from a variety of political perspectives were published on her actions and trial, in standard and abolitionist papers. A century later, Toni Morrison fictionalized and reinvented Garner's ordeal in the Nobel Prize–winning novel *Beloved* (1987), which Oprah made into a film, casting herself in the role of the infanticidal mother. *Beloved* is considered one of the most important literary reckonings with the legacy of slavery, and Garner's case a flash point foreshadowing the impending Civil War, seen by both abolitionist and proslavery advocates as proof of the correctness of their divergent viewpoints.

Garner was born enslaved on John Pollard Gaines's Maplewood plantation south of Covington, Kentucky. Gaines sold Maplewood to his brother Archibald Gaines in 1849 when he was appointed to the governorship of the Oregon Territory. At the time of the sale,

Garner was sixteen years old, pregnant, and about to marry Robert Garner, who was enslaved on a neighboring plantation. During the six years she worked as a domestic in Archibald Gaines's home, Garner bore four children, at least two of which had light complexions and were assumed to have a white father. Garner served as a wet nurse for Archibald's wife and babies during the same time period her own babies needed breast milk. Severe scarring on Garner's face was viewed as evidence of the harsh conditions at Maplewood.

On January 26, 1856, the Garners escaped across the frozen Ohio River into Cincinnati and stopped briefly at a cabin that served as a way station for the Underground Railroad. Before they could continue north, however, marshals acting under the authority of the federal Fugitive Slave Act of 1850 surrounded the cabin and endeavored to take the Garners into custody by force. Margaret is reported to have panicked and tried to slaughter all of her children before the marshals could break into the cabin, slashing her four- and six-year-old sons with a knife and hitting her infant daughter with a shovel while the children and other members of her family begged her to stop. She then slit the throat of her two-year-old daughter, Mary, her rumored favorite, killing her.[55]

What we know of Garner comes from a series of judicial hearings and newspaper reports after she was brought into custody. The timing of her personal tragedy made her case an irresistible example for abolitionists and proslavery advocates to draw upon in legal and moral debates. The arguments made at her trial eerily predict the impending national crisis. John Jolliffe, an abolitionist attorney, represented Garner and initially attempted to put forward an argument about states' rights in order to prevent Gaines from transporting Garner back into slavery in Kentucky. Jolliffe mounted a direct attack on the legitimacy of the fugitive slave statute and insisted that both Garners had been to Ohio previously, which established their claim to freedom. The court quickly rebuffed this argument, which prompted Jolliffe to attempt a more creative attack on the immorality of the Fugitive Slave Act, describing slavery as a "roaring, seething, hissing Hell."[56] With armed mobs of proslavery and abolitionist forces clashing in the streets outside the courthouse and many abolitionists in attendance at the trial, Jolliffe asserted that the Fugitive Slave Act violated the right to religious freedom because it coerced those with faith-based objections to slavery to go against their beliefs and assist with returning slaves to their masters. This argument was also quickly rejected by the court.

There is no recorded testimony from Garner. Instead, on February 13, 1856, after the formal proceedings concluded, prominent Bostonian feminist and abolitionist Lucy Stone was granted permission to speak on Garner's behalf from the judge's desk. She was reported to have spent a great deal of time with the Garners while they were in custody, yet her characterization of Garner deployed familiar sentiments and stereotypes. Stone described Garner as a "victim" whose "lip quivered in silent agony"—a description that invoked natural maternal affection and grief, emotions usually attributed only to white mothers. Even more boldly, Stone repeatedly compared Garner to the revolutionary soldiers, insisting that if it was a "good deed to give a weapon to those who fought the battle of liberty on Bunker's Hill—if those patriots had the right to use the arms supplied to them—she who said: 'Let us go to God rather than go back to slavery,' had the same right. . . . Who that knows the depth of a mother's love does not estimate the sacrifice she had made? If she had a right to deliver her child, she had a right to deliver herself. So help me heaven! I would tear from myself my life with my teeth, before I would be a slave!"[57] Stone's cause was virtuous and urgent, and it is understandable that she would aim for the most persuasive rhetoric possible. Yet her comparison cast Garner's act of desperation and panic as a righteous, intentional feat of resistance, overlooking that Garner's actual victim was her own two-year old daughter, not the institution of slavery. Stone further claimed that she had convinced Gaines to free Garner after her return to Maplewood by telling him "that his name would be connected with the events now occurring; with execration, if he continued to enslave one capable of such deeds as this woman; but with honour, if he gave the freedom that was her right."[58] Stone's remarks were published in the *Liberator* and distributed nationally. For proslavery advocates, including Gaines, however, the violence of Garner's actions was proof that enslaved women lacked maternal affection and needed the protection afforded by slavery. Despite Stone's public assurance that she had won the family's freedom, the Garners were transported back to Kentucky under Gaines's ownership.

Garner was not prosecuted for her daughter's murder. Archibald sold her and her surviving children, who had remained in her care, to another plantation further south and arranged for the family to be transported there by boat. While on the water, Garner attempted to drown her children, but again failed.

In the absence of any record of Emerson's, Clifton's, Jenkins's, or Garner's thoughts and feelings as their cases proceeded, all four situations, including the women's motives, are to some extent unknowable to contemporary readers. Emerson's testimony was recorded immediately after she had delivered twins alone, while she was still recovering from the birth. She may have been experiencing the hopelessness of postpartum depression as she navigated her doomed defense alone, terrified of her abusive parents and the magistrate. Perhaps she chose to convey a version of events most tolerable to her psyche at the time. Clifton might have endeavored to appear as a "mute slave" and Jenkins as submissive, or the court records and press coverage of both women may have shaped them to conform to stereotypes.

While much scholarly attention has focused on trying to understand women's motives for committing infanticide, the sources that are available on the historical record offer more concrete evidence of the motives of the more empowered actors who inserted themselves into high-profile infant homicide trials. Mather's sermon on uncleanliness and parental authority occasioned by Emerson's hanging and Stone's abolitionist remarks at the end of Garner's trial are but two notable examples of how empowered social actors can capitalize on the publicity of a sensational infant homicide case to elaborate their own religious and political ambitions.

On the opposite end of the social hierarchy from Mather and Stone, a disproportionally large number of women who faced public accusations of infanticide lived and worked as domestic servants in close quarters with other servants. This trend appears by the end of the nineteenth century and persisted into the twentieth. These tragedies speak volumes about the restrictive norms governing motherhood at the time, which disallowed these women from claiming the status and performing the role of mother.[59] This population was certainly uniquely burdened by out-of-wedlock pregnancy, which could reveal an affair or rape within the household and would lead to immediate unemployment and homelessness. Even still, domestic servants are overrepresented in the court documents and jail logs, likely due to their lack of access to privacy and their lack of family support and supervision. Family members with interconnected fates would have been more highly motivated to help care for a newborn or even help commit and conceal an infanticide. Irish historians have detailed cases where family members encouraged and assisted with killing illegitimate babies. In one instance, a pregnant woman's mother sent her a packet of poison powder and instructions on how to administer it.[60]

Irish historian Cliona Rattigan has also documented a pattern of preemptive community surveillance of domestic servants who were suspected of concealing illegitimate pregnancies that lasted into the 1930s.[61] In these cases, those living in closest proximity kept careful watch, informing law enforcement of concealed pregnancies well ahead of births, and then arriving on the scene to catch women in the act of committing infanticide. Emerson's case presents a much earlier example of this kind of preemptive surveillance and community-level enforcement in the United States. Community members appear to have prioritized protecting social norms and religious values over extending help to women and babies in crisis. These women's isolation and marginalization harmed their babies.

The neglectful treatment of women faced with problem pregnancies in the past is, in part, a reflection of their lack of social standing as well as the lack of status afforded babies, especially illegitimate babes, at that time. This kind of negligent treatment was supported ideologically by myths about maternal affection that persist into the present; mothers assume sole responsibility for their offspring and their affectionate, safe care is taken for granted—no matter what is happening in the mother's life. The many echoes between the historical cases described here and the treatment of contemporary cases, like Emile's, raise damning questions about how much, or more accurately how little, has changed. Like Emerson, Emile too faced preemptive community surveillance without the benefit of proactive intervention. Like Emerson, Emile too was judged based on her perceived failure to conform to unrealistic maternal ideals immediately post-partum.

These maternal myths also help explain the lack of attention to child welfare in the archive of sources left on the historical record documenting infanticide. Garner's children remained in her care after her violent assault on them, and Clifton and the many other accused women who were not convicted likely went on to raise children too. The physical remains of newborns found in early American cities and smaller towns show a wide range of parental conduct. Many of the babies found abandoned after death due to the prohibitive cost of securing a cemetery burial were tucked into handmade coffins, wrapped in special clothes and garments, and left with emblems of affection. Other infant corpses, however, show signs of unnecessarily extreme violence. Babies were found bound to rocks at the bottom of riverways and burned to the bones, others with stab wounds, bludgeoning blows, near decapitations, and other signs of mutilation. There are a handful of cases in the historical record of men being punished for violent infant homicides; none have been the subject of in-depth investigation by historians. Looking back it is impossible to know now how many violent infant deaths occurred, let alone the percentage committed by men. As Clifton's and Garner's actions illustrate, however, mothers could also act with intense, horrific aggression. The signs of desperation or rage left on dead infants are perhaps the most difficult evidence to comprehend, because they so flatly contradict the dominant legal and cultural scripts that center women's victimization, shame, and submission as opposed to their terror or anger or powerful will for self-preservation.

CHAPTER 2

The Discovery of Heterogeneity

INTERDISCIPLINARY PERSPECTIVES ON MOTIVE, AGENCY, AND CULPABILITY

In May of 1969, a block from Miami Beach's white sand coastline, the American Psychiatric Association hosted its 125th Anniversary Meeting at the Americana and Balmoral hotels. Phillip J. Resnick, a medical resident at the time, gave a presentation at the conference on the findings from his first publications on the intersection of mental illness and fatal parental violence. Despite being new to the profession, Resnick introduced a framework for categorizing the motives of people who kill their children that would play a determining role in the next fifty years of research in his field. Where Dr. John Brodhead Beck applied his medical training to the development of forensics, Resnick at first drew on Rorschach tests and Freudian theory to analyze the interiority of mothers who kill. In doing so, he identified a key distinction between the psychology of parents who kill older babies and children and that of younger teenagers who kill newborns immediately at birth. To mark this distinction, Resnick coined a term to describe the latter group: "neonaticide."[1]

Resnick's framework marked a step forward in psychological understandings of infanticide beyond Beck's crude distinction between lewd and seduced. Yet his work also demonstrates how durable historical stereotypes of those who commit infanticide remain and how difficult it is to decenter them in scientific inquiry and legal practice, especially given their lucrative appeal in popular culture. Despite attracting critics from outside of forensic psychiatry, Resnick's early publications still endure as the most frequently cited on the subject. Given the significant impact of his work and the critiques that have been levied against it, this chapter takes an in-depth look at Resnick's early publications and professional practice, revealing his role in the emergence of a new politics of sympathy.

Since the early 2000s, researchers from a range of interdisciplinary fields, including feminist legal and cultural studies scholars, nurse practitioners, and psychiatrists specializing in women's mental and reproductive health, have worked toward a more contextualized understanding of neonaticide. Critical of mainstream forensic psychiatry's approach to categorizing types of offenders based on individual motives, researchers from outside of the field have uncovered key social, cultural, and biological drivers. Taking the lead on this novel line of inquiry, Michelle Oberman, an internationally recognized expert on law and women's reproductive health, argues that infanticide, historically and today, must be understood as a "response to the societal construction of and constraints on mothering."[2]

"Infanticide is not a random, unpredictable crime," writes Oberman. "Instead it is deeply embedded in, and responsive to, the societies in which it occurs" and is "committed by mothers who cannot parent their child under the circumstances dictated by their unique position in place and time."[3] Oberman argues that infanticide is a predicable, patterned act that is "readily understandable" once the everyday stressors that adhere to the norms dictating motherhood are identified.[4] With psychologist Cheryl Meyer, Oberman has analyzed newspaper accounts of infanticide and court filings in infanticide cases, interviewed women in prison, and, on occasion, testified on their behalf.[5] Oberman and Meyer are among the few researchers to document the personal narratives of women incarcerated for killing their children, outside of clinical evaluations. They are also the first researchers to reflect on their positionality in relation to these women and the many differences between these women's experiences of parenting and their own. Their analysis reveals the extent to which unresolved childhood trauma, sexual and domestic abuse, weak or nonexistent social ties, and substance abuse disorders factor into maternal killings, as well as the key preventative roles played by social and state support systems. The women whose lives they detail appear powerless—lacking enough agency in their lives to be held accountable for the choices they make. The most devastating conclusion from their prison interviews is that the presence of "one positive factor"—a decent paycheck, an empathetic friend, a trusted family member, a therapist, an affordable apartment, access to nonpunitive respite childcare, addiction treatment, sleep—could have saved lives.

Before diving into Resnick's backstory, it is important to pause and note the dearth of intellectual advancements on infanticide between Beck's work in the 1860s and Resnick's in the 1970s and to carefully review the few historical accounts from this period. While there is no systematic national account to draw on, it seems likely that rates of and motives driving infant homicide must have been impacted by two world wars, the Great Depression, shifts in the norms dictating sexuality, illegitimacy, access to birth control and abortion, and, eventually, the advent of pregnancy testing (around 1976) and DNA testing (around 1986). The beginning of the twentieth century marked a period of sweeping demographic change, as large populations of rural and immigrant young women moved into urban centers and lived and worked without family support or supervision for the first time. Urbanization and industrialization created new opportunities for recreation and novel sexual economies that spiked unplanned, unwanted pregnancies, presenting survival challenges for young women who were paid less than subsistence wages and whose futures were largely dictated by opportunities for marriage.[6] These constrained circumstances created a context within which infanticide likely endured as a survival strategy, with the conditions that put domestic servants at risk in the nineteenth century carrying over to women working in cities in the twentieth.

A rare article written in 1959 by Lester Adelson, a coroner, noted that street cleaners, trash collectors, and sewer workers continued to routinely encounter the corpses of dead babies. Adelson lamented his inability to identify perpetrators, even in cases where infants were discovered with multiple stab wounds. To emphasize this point, he includes a black and white photograph of a newborn baby girl curled in a loose fetal pose whose neck and chest bear the mark of thirty-three superficial and deep stab wounds. The infant was attacked by its eighteen-year-old mother immediately after birth while the placenta was still in her body. She was discovered by her mother bleeding vaginally, who insisted her daughter could not have been pregnant because she was "certain [her daughter] was not the kind of girl who would get in that kind of trouble."[7]

Despite indications of its continued prevalence, however, historical accounts of infanticide in the United States during the twentieth century are almost nonexistent. No national historical study of the practice exists. Instead, there are a handful of surprising case studies that shed light on specific communities in discrete locations over brief time spans from the end of the nineteenth century to the first half of the twentieth. This historical period, during which class, race, and racism shaped the choices available to women with problem pregnancies, includes the rise of Victorian sensibilities at the end of the nineteenth century that heightened the stigma associated with illegitimacy among middle- and upper-class white women. These women would have been likely to travel to give birth to babies out of wedlock and then abandon them far from family,[8] but, by the twentieth century, many also had access to maternity and foundling homes and an organized, if extralegal, adoption network. Looking at the segregated landscape of maternity services in Richmond, Virginia, social historian Elna Green observes that, amid a lack of options, "black women more often found themselves with no choice but to leave their infants exposed." Infanticide, like "lynching," Green concludes, was "a form of violence shaped by racism."[9]

The fact that infanticide and infant abandonment in the United States are so poorly documented suggests an assumption on the part of mainstream historians that these were marginal, insignificant concerns—an unjustified one given rigorous documentation by non-American historians of infant homicide and abandonment in, for example, Great Britain.[10] A close reading of the limited social history demonstrates that these tragedies were central to many women's lives and indicative of their struggle to survive and lack of status. Green critiques historians of the New South between 1880 and 1910 who "chronicled in great detail the growth of industries, the expansion of cities, and the motives of the men who made it all happen," while ignoring the poor and the marginal: "When seen from the very bottom of the social order, the New South does not appear so 'bustling' and 'vigorous.' To poor women and their babies, Richmond's struggle to modernize, diversify, and industrialize carried a terrible cost. Growing Streetcar lines might be one symbol of the New South. A 'Potter's Field' overcrowded with tiny caskets was another."[11] Green's description of Richmond's largest African American cemetery "overcrowded with tiny caskets" underscores that infant mortality and infanticide persisted into the twentieth century as a central fact of life for many. Bearing witness to the precarious lives of marginalized parents and babies alters the national historical narrative in disturbing, necessary ways. Telling the story of U.S. infanticide likely remains taboo in part because it so horrifyingly undermines any sense of American exceptionalism.

In the first half of the twentieth century, despite sweeping social, cultural, and economic changes, women from a wide range of different backgrounds in numerous countries continued to find themselves with few, if any, options when faced with a pregnancy that might undercut their social standing, or destroy their marriage prospects, or uncover incest or rape, or prompt immediate unemployment, or threaten the survival of their older children. During this period, lawmakers in Canada, Australia, New Zealand, and many European countries began to take notice of these fraught circumstances. Politicians in these countries tried to address the mismatch between outdated laws, which mandated the death sentence for women convicted of infanticide, and almost all jurors' sympathy for the accused and unwillingness to convict, which stemmed from an awareness of the difficulties mothers endured. Politicians in Britain acted early to address this predicament by passing the 1922 Infanticide Act, defining infanticide as akin to manslaughter, a lesser offense than homicide, and granting women who killed newborns while still psychologically and physically impacted by childbirth and lactation either lenient sentencing or hospitalization instead of imprisonment. British doctors and psychiatrists at the time largely agreed that pregnancy and the postpartum period were riddled with mental health risks, including so-called lactational insanity, and that the physical strain of repeated pregnancies on impoverished women could trigger "exhaustion psychosis." In 1938, lawmakers expanded the protections of the 1922 act beyond women who killed newborns at birth to include women who killed babies anytime during the first year of life. Though these updated laws, which are still in place, universally define women who kill babies as mentally ill, depriving them of agency no matter the specifics of their cases, they benefit the accused through more consistent sentencing and a higher standard of proof for convictions. The maximum sentence for infanticide ranges from one to five years, with imprisonment reserved for exceptional cases.

In the United States, there was no comparable legislative debate. Today infant homicide is prosecuted under the same laws that govern homicide among adults. Several cases from the first half of the twentieth century reveal that colonial-era legal norms and nineteenth-century stereotypes persisted in the absence of distinct infanticide legislation, but also that the same public sympathy that inspired leniency and legislative change abroad still dictated actual sentencing norms in the United States, in all but rare cases where mothers were perceived as unusually callous or cunning. Even as religious officials and the popular press loudly condemned women who killed their children, public sympathy reigned—except in rare cases such as those of Lucinda Riendeau and Evelyn Bullock. These cases illustrate that professionals working in the criminal justice system continued to rely on snap judgments about women's character and performance of maternal affection well into the 1930s and beyond. By virtue of offering both victim and villain categories, sympathy and condemnation stemmed from the same historical stereotypes and tropes.

Lucinda Riendeau of Providence, Rhode Island, bore no direct culpability for the murder of her baby. Her husband, George, had forced her to send their firstborn to a boarding house so that she could continue working; when Riendeau insisted on keeping their second son at home, George poisoned the baby with arsenic.

Historian Simone Caron writes that Riendeau "did not present herself as a model mother grieving over her child" after police found the vial of arsenic in George's pocket; "she was too eager to see her husband jailed," which would have liberated her from his abuse and perhaps allowed her to reunite with her first child. "This sense of control over her life may have veiled her sorrow," considers Caron, "but the coroner ignored these mitigating circumstances" and instead based his judgment on her failure to appear properly grief-stricken, his inquest finding Riendeau "criminally responsible."[12]

In 1934, Evelyn Bullock, also of Providence, was a teen living at home and working as a wood vendor with her brother. While out making deliveries, she fell ill and asked to use the restroom in a client's restaurant. She emerged after thirty minutes, thanked the owner, and returned to making deliveries. The restaurant owner later found her dead newborn and called the authorities. Bullock and her family told investigators that they were unaware of the pregnancy; Bullock explained that she had spotted throughout the previous months and that her body had not changed noticeably. These details suggest that Bullock either did not recognize her pregnancy or relied on denial to cope; she did not experience what are considered the hallmark symptoms of pregnancy and, in the absence of those signs, her family either became complicit in her denial or also simply did not perceive the situation accurately. Impregnated by her brother-in-law, she also confessed to not wanting the baby.

But "despite her youth, birthing alone, and claims of insanity," Caron writes, Bullock "garnered no sympathy" from the coroner in her case, who relied on the assessment of the restaurant owner after his thirty-second exchange with Bullock: "She appeared to me like a 'tough nut'[;] she was not quiet and nice. She never said a word beyond thanking me for the use of my sanitary place." Perhaps he disapproved of the overalls Bullock wore to perform manual labor.

(In contrast, a patron of the restaurant told investigators that Bullock had "acted quietly.") Relying on widespread, classist assumptions about proper maternal behavior, the coroner ruled that Bullock possessed "no mother love or affection, not even the consideration that one of the lesser strata would have for its own" and found her criminally responsible for the death of her newborn.[13]

The punitive outcome of Bullock's and Riendeau's cases was unusual for the time period. Yet these cases underscore that the same stereotypes used to distinguish between blameless and blameworthy perpetrators that characterized earlier infanticide trials persisted into the twentieth century; Emile's case reveals that these stereotypes continue to be deployed today. The primacy of coroners' and prosecutors' discretion in the absence of infanticide-specific legislation in determining which infant homicides are investigated and how they are punished also continues to this day, with little consistency or logic. These determinations are also influenced heavily by the opinions of those living and working in closest proximity to the accused, who may be the only ones with access to evidence of an infant homicide, especially a neonaticide. Factors including visible signs of violence on the infant's corpse, the mother's preparations for the baby's arrival, age, previous experiences with childbirth, and the results of the floating lung test have been and remain standard considerations, though emphasized inconsistently. In this chaotic context, Leona Maciejkowicz's case is representative of the broader twentieth-century public and judicial tendency to sympathize with women who kill newborns, albeit in ways that relegate them to the roles of either victim or mental health patient.

In 1937 Maciejkowicz was an unmarried twenty-one-year-old living in Hamtramck, Michigan, a Detroit suburb with a large Polish immigrant community. At first she confessed to stabbing her newborn with a comb at birth, prompting local newspapers to run front-page headlines branding her a "Baby Killer." During her initial trial, however, Maciejkowicz recanted her confession, insisting that she had been unaware of the pregnancy until heavy labor set in while she was taking a bath alone in her rooming house. "In pain and distress," historian Karen Majewski writes, Maciejkowicz hurried to clean up by wrapping the dead infant in newspaper and placing it in a drawer in time to make the start of her shift at the Bohn Aluminum Company.[14] Like many other women in this dire circumstance, Maciejkowicz's shock and dissociation led to oddly ambivalent treatment of the infant's corpse and an adrenaline-driven feat of postdelivery normalcy. Both seemingly inexplicable behaviors are themes across accounts of historical and contemporary neonaticides and speak to the underlying biology of shock, which is but one consequence of the many medical injuries that can occur as a result of unassisted childbirth.

The jury convicted Maciejkowicz of second-degree murder, but the judge intervened, and the devoutly Catholic Polish community rallied in her defense. Given the official doctrine of their religion, support from Catholic women might seem counterintuitive. Yet women in this community were well-versed in the difficulty of mothering under adverse circumstances and with few resources. Letters sent to the popular radio show of Polish American priest Father Justin Figas document his listeners' intimate knowledge of the survival challenges faced by overburdened mothers. When Figas told stories designed to shame women for seeking out birth control and abortion, his listeners responded with indignation: "Doesn't my health mean anything?" one mother asked. Another detailed how her mother, raising six children while married to an abusive alcoholic, "got old before her time." The listener's mother died at sixty-five. "What was the use of living that long?" she asks Figas. "She never had proper clothing, never had time to leave the house for a visit, never had money for the dentist, because there were so many of us kids."[15] As these letters reveal, official censure meant little in the face of bare necessity.

In Maciejkowicz's second trial, granted by and then presided over by the same judge, she was allowed to plead guilty to manslaughter, a charge that allowed for more leniency. The judge, noting that he had "never seen a girl who has gone through such hardship," sentenced her to two years of probation under the care of social worker and political activist Lottie Ostrowski, whose husband was the director of the Hamtramck Department of Public Works. "Let us hope that everybody will join together in aiding her," the judge added. "She deserves a chance." Hamtramck policewomen, Polish clubs, and "scores of Hamtramck and North Detroit women" joined the chorus in defense of the "poor Polish girl," who was reported to have lost her mother as a toddler (or perhaps teenager, as other accounts suggested), submitting petitions calling for her release. The sympathy extended to Maciejkowicz in the press was also remarkable in its intensity: "Local citizens are giving her the rest and peace of mind she so richly deserves," remarked *The Hamtramck New Deal*; the *Detroit Medical News* editorialized that Maciejkowicz's crime was "understandable" given her circumstances and mental state and called on the community to ensure that "this girl, hardly a woman in years" should receive "all sympathy, and kindness, and consideration in her sickness." "She is not on trial," the *Medical News* concluded. "It is society that should do groveling penance."[16]

The arbitrary assignment of culpability versus insanity, punishment versus sympathy, that characterized Bullock's, Riendeau's, and Maciejkowicz's cases and that persists into present-day legal practice is a key context for understanding both the purpose of Resnick's framework as well as the trajectory of research on infanticide from the twentieth into the twenty-first century. Much like Beck and other nineteenth-century practitioners of state medicine, Resnick and other researchers in his field would lay the groundwork for forensic psychiatry by attempting to inform prosecutorial discretion with empirical observation.

Resnick's central insight was that the motives of parents who purposefully kill older children are fundamentally different from the motives of mothers who kill newborns at birth. The former are significantly more impaired by severe mental illness and more likely to be driven by a slurry of suicidal and altruistic ambitions—such as believing, accurately or not, that the child is suffering or that it is in the child's best interest to ascend to heaven before the parent's suicide rather than face damnation alone. In contrast, teenagers and young adults who kill babies immediately at birth may be trapped by an unwanted pregnancy in an untenable context but do not typically lack sanity—outside of the time-specific mental health impacts associated with unassisted childbirth, which are not recognized in the *Diagnostic and Statistical Manual of Mental Disorders*, fifth edition (DSM-5-TR), the American Psychiatric Association's classification of mental disorders. Resnick argued that, in these cases, women's primary motive was "simply not wanting" the baby and coined the term "neonaticide" to describe them. The distinction Resnick marked with the term is an enduringly salient one, borne out in the most recent child and infant homicide statistics in the United States, which point to a unique period of vulnerability to homicide during the first day of life. Resnick's claim that these tragedies occur because the mother does not desire the baby has been widely critiqued, however;[17] other researchers argue that such actions are instead "rooted in shock, disabling terror, shame, and guilt."[18]

The research Resnick shared in Miami shifted the trajectory of his professional life. In 1976 he began leading the Court Psychiatric Clinic of Cleveland, which evaluates approximately 3,000 felons per year; as of 2024, he continues to supervise and teach for the Forensic Psychiatry Fellowship at Case School of Medicine and see patients as the Director of Forensic Psychiatry at UH Cleveland Medical Center. Resnick's unique areas of expertise, including translating psychological insights in legal contexts, have earned him a national stage on numerous occasions: Resnick consulted on the high-profile cases of Jeffrey Dahmer, Susan Smith, Timothy McVeigh, Andrea Yates, Scott Peterson, Casey Anthony, James Holmes, and Theodore Kaczynski, the Unabomber. He served as the president of the American Academy of Psychiatry and the Law and is the lead author on over 200 articles and book chapters.

Resnick's original interest in understanding women like Susan Smith and Andrea Yates was a matter of dark happenstance paired with professional ambition and personal sympathy.[19] While serving in the Army after completing his medical degree, ultimately attaining the rank of captain, Resnick spent the second of two years of on-the-job medical training leading a women's inpatient unit at Valley Forge Hospital. Within a one-month period, Resnick admitted two military wives who had taken their children's lives. A third woman, admitted later, revealed that she had killed her newborn at birth nineteen years earlier, and became the central case report for Resnick's article on neonaticide.

Resnick shared these women's stories with me when I spoke with him over Zoom in late August 2023 to better understand his practice outside of his publications and the backstory on his seminal 1969–1970 articles. When I read Resnick for the first time in the early 2010s, as both a new PhD and new mother, I had been critical of how his landmark studies lump cases from hundreds of years of human history and geography into a single framework. I had found the implication that mothers' motives had remained static in the face of seismic medical, social, and economic changes reductive. I had also bristled at Resnick's claim that infant victims in homicide cases are "simply not wanted," which seemed to conflate the rationales for seeking abortion with the drive toward neonaticide—neither of which seem to me, then or now, to be simply a matter of wanting or not wanting—and to do a disservice to the complexity of both.

In conversation with him, however, I realized that the categories of motive Resnick lays out in his publications are a pragmatic diagnostic tool tailored to our legal system's requirements; in his professional practice, he pays careful attention to each individual's unique psychology, the quality of their intimate relationships, and other highly variable life circumstances and statuses. For rare cases in which women act with intention, malice, and aggression, Resnick is careful to make sure his professional insights will land with a lay audience of jurors, describing the women as "tough cookies"—an echo of the terms applied to Bullock in the 1930s, and the colonial-era rhetoric of lewd and cunning. Other, more common, cases that Resnick has assessed are instead tragic accidents or immature mistakes.

One of the military wives Resnick examined had been stationed in Alaska, where daylight lasted a mere four hours during the winter months and light-induced depression was common. Her actions stemmed from a biological response to her environment, layered with sleep deprivation and postpartum hormonal shifts known to trigger depression. The second military wife had been stationed in Italy. She and her husband both knew that she could not manage the difficulty of caring for a third child and therefore sought a tubal ligation, which required the approval of a military psychiatrist who could confirm that pregnancy would threaten the mother's life. The psychiatrist approved the procedure, but the only obstetrician who could perform it refused to do so. Prior to receiving Resnick's patient's request, the same obstetrician had sterilized a different mother of two healthy children. Horrifically, after their mother's procedure, both children drowned while playing outside together on thin ice. The obstetrician's guilt after this tragedy meant that Resnick's patient was denied access to needed birth control. After delivering her third child, Resnick's patient fell into the severe depression that she and her husband had anticipated with dread. She killed all three of their children.

Resnick learned that the psychiatrist who had assessed the mother who was denied a tubal ligation had published a case report on her tragedy. Resnick's advisor encouraged him to do the same. Instead of merely writing up another report, however, Resnick embarked on a review of the "world literature from 1751 to 1968" to find past infanticide cases. In an era before search engines and online databases, Resnick sifted by hand through a paper copy of the Index Medica, a bibliographic complication of scientific articles with its own indexing language. He found articles with titles such as "Female Criminal Lunatics: A Sketch" and "Eskimo Infanticide" in thirteen languages, written by psychiatrists both in public practice and in prisons, coroners, and staff at mental hospitals. Now in his residency, Resnick secured $1,200 to hire translators for the French and German studies and reviewed each publication until he had amassed an archive of 167 case reports, 131 filicide cases, and 36 neonaticides. He then assigned a motive to each case "based on the explanation given by the murderer" and, he says, "independent of diagnosis."[20] These motives then became the basis for a framework that generations of forensic psychiatrists would follow, publishing numerous reviews of basically the same literature that only slightly modify Resnick's original categories.

While Resnick insists that his examination of the reports was conducted at a clinical remove, the nature of his sources suggests that his framework is an amalgamation of historically ingrained stereotypes from the world literature layered with subtle observations from his practice. These are not deathbed confessions or diary entries; they are professional assessments, demonstrating how the experts who encountered these women and men chose to explain their motives to other experts. One can imagine the pressure, even terror, those accused may have felt during these high-stakes moments of judgment in which a stranger wielded influence over the duration of their looming confinement or the severity of their criminal punishment, judging their culpability for what is widely viewed as an unspeakably repulsive crime.

The layering of astute firsthand observations onto historical stereotypes is most apparent in Resnick's original article on neonaticide for *The American Journal of Psychiatry.* The article reveals numerous, diverse reasons why neonaticides occur and puts forward a novel politics of sympathy for women based on their guilt and grief, rather than, as nineteenth-century doctors and lawmakers would have advocated, the presumed shame wrought by male seduction and abandonment: "Each neonaticide is tragic," Resnick stated, "not only for the infant but also for the continuing effect that the crime has on the life of the mother."[21]

Resnick's new politics of sympathy, however, is built on top of a dichotomy that echoes the approach of Beck and his contemporaries. Resnick notes that the extant literature parses women who kill illegitimate babies at birth into "two major groups." The first highly sympathetic cohort includes "delicate," "passive," "unwed girls" who know "the value of a chaste reputation" and tragically sacrifice "what on more fortunate occasions, it would have been their pride to cherish." "Strong instinctual drives and little ethical restraint" define women in the second group, who tend to be "older, strong willed, and often promiscuous." For these women, neonaticide is "usually premediated and not out of keeping with their previous lifestyle."

While Resnick doesn't use the word "cunning," the description of women in this second category, who willfully plan to assassinate their newborns to maintain their "lifestyle," echoes Cotton Mather's sermon at Elizabeth Emerson's hanging.[22]

In synthesizing the extant research literature, Resnick inevitably ran into long-standing stereotypes that create narrow, predictable boxes; from 1770 to 1970 in white middle- and upper-class circles, the stigmatization of premarital sex and illegitimacy appears to have persisted in ways that overdetermined how infanticide was understood and represented. During our interview, Resnick remembered that it was common for young pregnant women in the 1950s through 1970s to be secreted away to Florence Crittenton homes, clandestine maternity facilities, where their babies would be adopted at birth to shield their families from social rejection. A *Washington Post* article on these homes states that in just the two decades preceding the legalization of abortion, an estimated 1.5 million American women "were forced to have their babies and give them up for adoption." These "mostly white, middle-class teens and young women," the article explains, "were systematically shamed, hidden in maternity homes and then coerced into handing over their children to adoption agencies without being informed of their legal rights."[23]

The widespread reliance on covert maternity homes and forced, secret adoptions is an important backdrop for the case report Resnick details in his article on neonaticide. The subject, Mrs. C., was a "thirty-six-year-old married, childless secretary" when she was admitted to Resnick's inpatient unit. Resnick describes Mrs. C's troubled childhood, noting her father's affairs and her feelings of being unable to earn her mother's approval. He details her first memory of being taken out in a new dress at the age of three to be "shown off" by her father to other men who joked that "she was too cute to be his." Even after her parents separated permanently, her father still returned home to have Mrs. C. "launder his shirts," a detail Resnick finds significant. He speculates that "Mrs. C. may have failed to reveal her pregnancy to her mother because of the unconscious idea that it would be viewed as proof of incest."[24]

"Unresolved oedipal feelings" or otherwise, Mrs. C explained to Resnick that her relationship at the age of seventeen with the father of her child had been brief, and that she had "passively submitted to sexual relations to avoid his disapproval." "Certain she could never let her mother know," Mrs. C. corseted herself throughout the pregnancy and retreated to a bathroom when labor set in while she was home alone. After the birth, which Resnick does not describe, she "strangled the infant with her hands" and "hung it on a towel rack with a hanger until she had cleaned up. She wrapped the body in old clothes and put it in a dresser drawer overnight. The next day she put it in the rubbish." In the moment, she explained that she was stunned by her own calmness and that the actions she took felt like "just something that had to be done."[25]

Later, however, the crime haunted her. She strove to "do good" in an attempt to "even things up," but her remorse left her in what Resnick diagnosed as a "psychotic depression." Her symptoms included severe weight loss, insomnia, indecisiveness, and an inability to concentrate. Four months before she would attempt suicide, "Mrs. C. found a letter indicating that her husband had been unfaithful," Resnick recounts. "As with each previous adversity she encountered, she felt that this was retribution for her killing." Eventually, "she became totally preoccupied with how 'evil' she was, especially because of her neonaticide. Feeling that she deserved to die, she drank a glass of corrosive liquid," damaging her throat as she had damaged her baby's.[26]

Reflecting on these early encounters with mothers who kill their children, Resnick recalls confronting bias within the health care system, even among his own nursing staff. "I felt affection and very much empathic to each of these women who were severely depressed at the time they did this," he says, but had trouble finding civilian facilities who would accept them:

> The first reaction I got was "Oh, we're not going to take anyone that killed their own child." It was so stigmatizing that it was very difficult to be able to transfer them. I recall that it was a major task.
>
> And later in my career when I was at my own university hospital and teaching, when I admitted a woman who had killed her children, again the nurses were very angry. "Why are you admitting these monsters to the hospital?"
>
> However, once they were admitted, and the nurses became acquainted with their circumstance, they ended up being very fond of these women and empathic. But in the abstract, they sound like horrible people. When the nurses got to know them, they were glad to have them on the unit.[27]

In sharing these struggles, Resnick makes clear the purpose of distinguishing between women who commit filicide and neonaticide: to discern who can be helped most by the mental health care system and who is most in need of, and empirically justified in seeking, an insanity defense.

Many women who commit filicide seek out mental health care prior to harming their children. Their suicidal and homicidal thoughts are terrifying. Mothers experiencing nonpsychotic postpartum depression are more likely to volunteer suicidal thoughts than infanticidal ones—even though the fear of harming their babies is the reason they seek out mental health care.[28] Doctors and psychiatrists need to be prepared to probe, carefully. Given that multiple lives are at stake, inpatient care should be utilized more preemptively than might be the case for others with suicidal ideation. Women who commit filicide are also more likely to be afflicted by a mental illness that is already recognized in the DSM-5-TR and thus by the American court system than women who commit neonaticide. This is an important area of current research. Experts on women's reproductive mental health, primarily Dr. Diana Barnes, call for pregnancy denial, now more accurately described as "unperceived pregnancy," to be added to the manual.[29] While filicide is driven by a diversity of motives, the backstories behind the Alaskan and Italian cases reveal that there are good reasons to be optimistic that these tragedies may be prevented—*if* women's birth control and family planning needs are respected and *if* they have access to mental health care. Neonaticide is the more intractable tragedy.

As a discipline, forensic psychiatry is embedded within and thus is a tool of the criminal justice system. Researchers in this tradition, like Resnick, seek to apply scientific insights to legal practice and generate empathy through an understanding of mental health. By contrast, efforts by sociological and medical researchers to identify risk factors—from unresolved childhood trauma and weak social ties to a biological, somatic basis for unperceived pregnancies—are not inherently about assessing motive. This research supports an empathetic understanding of women who kill their own babies without considering them either victims or insane, and points to numerous possible policy avenues for improving prevention. Yet it also reveals how intractable these tragedies remain and how even empathy can be shaded by stereotypes that obscure the staggering diversity of those involved in these cases.

Meyer and Oberman's 2008 book, *When Mothers Kill: Interviews from Prison*, is a key contribution to this research. Working with a small team of collaborators, the authors conducted two rounds of in-depth, structured interviews with mothers incarcerated in the

Ohio Reformatory for Women (ORW) for killing one or more of their children: two- to three-hour-long interviews with forty women by Meyer, then, with Oberman, reinterviews of eight women. The researchers discovered that the majority of the women's children had died accidentally as a result of neglect and abuse, an important finding that reveals a shared set of risk factors—histories of family violence, addiction disorder, and everyday survival struggles—between women and men. In the absence of intent, infant and child deaths from abuse or neglect by both women and men appear to be driven by a lack of emotional preparation for parenting and a lack of resources and social supports.

In telling these women's tragic stories, Meyer and Oberman explode the monster mom myth. They analyze each interviewee's relationship with her mother and romantic partners and her experiences of mothering and of incarceration. The image of these women's lives that emerges is devastating: common themes include childhood sexual abuse that was ignored by family members; parental addiction disorder; severe physical and emotional abuse; feeling like an outsider within one's own family due to not being the biological offspring of the father figure; and yearning for the unconditional love a baby represents while being financially and emotionally unprepared for the realities of mothering. Meyer and Oberman identify exposure to violence, isolation, and hopelessness as a cornerstone in the lives of the women they interviewed.

The sheer scope of the horror and despair that have characterized these women's lives humbles Meyer and Oberman, who reflect on the disparity between "the awesome grace and bounty in our lives"[30] and their interviewees: "Our life experiences were so distinct as to render ambiguous even seemingly clear words, such as 'home' and 'good'"—several women, for example, describe "happy" childhoods in homes that are revealed to be "rife with violence."[31]

They conclude that enduring a single day of these women's childhoods would be "soul-crushing" and that their adult lives seem "hollow," without "even the hope for change."[32]

Meyer and Oberman conclude that their interviewees' struggles to parent with too few resources "offers a silent testimony to the fragile network that holds life together for the vast majority of mothers and children in society,"[33] and to the cruelty for society's most vulnerable mothers and babies of presuming that maternal altruism is innate. The notion that anyone could parent safely in the face of the emotional burdens and in the absence of resources these women navigate is impractical if not absurd.

Meyer and Oberman's argument has radical implications. In shifting attention away from women's character and morality and directing it toward their relationships and circumstances, their work undercuts the logic of criminal punishment, which they conclude offers little hope of deterrence or retribution. Prevention and punishment, from this angle, are unrelated. A society genuinely eager to save babies' lives needs an immediate investment in the social safety net writ large, as well as sweeping interventions to improve access to addiction disorder treatment, intra-family violence mitigation and parenting education, and affordable housing and childcare.

In critiquing the logic of punishment, Meyer and Oberman emphasize the powerlessness of their research participants. The stories they share are shaped by a state of choicelessness in which one wonders to what extent these women exerted any agency at all—many were barely surviving when they killed their children; many could easily have been killed themselves as children. I do not question if this is an accurate representation of the interviewees' lives—the evidence Meyer and Oberman present is as persuasive as it is painful. I do wonder, however, if this state of powerlessness and the degree to which their interviewees have been punished for their actions is specific to the population, rather than representative of these tragedies as a whole. Many women who face potential infant homicide charges elicit sympathy from health care workers, child welfare agents, and police and evade further investigation. Others are able to secure effective legal counsel. The fact that the women held in the ORW did not have even a single friend they could call for help or a family member in whom they could confide underscores their profound isolation. Perhaps Meyer and Oberman reveal more about the inequality that defines the criminal justice system than any universal experience of women who kill their offspring.

The studies described in this chapter were principally aimed at discerning the individual psychological patterns and social and cultural norms that drive infanticide. Discoveries by nurse practitioners, neuroscientists, and psychiatrists working on the frontlines of maternity care and reproductive mental health, however, have exposed a perplexing biological component behind certain unperceived pregnancies, which creates neonaticide risk in the absence of conscious motivation. Where Meyer and Oberman identify powerlessness as a factor, practitioner-scholars, focused on different populations, have instead pointed to choicelessness caused by an absence of conscious awareness. The difference arises from the population of research subjects; where Meyer and Oberman focused on women incarcerated for killing their children, research on unperceived pregnancy includes many who receive help and thus avoid harming their babies.

Importantly, this new, still small body of medical research concludes that it is impossible for a single framework or grand theory to encompass all infanticide cases, given their heterogeneity and that women do not share one universal experience of what it is like to be pregnant. The myth that pregnancy always looks and feels a certain way can convince certain pregnant women who do not experience these symptoms that they are not pregnant, which can create crisis pregnancy situations and accidental neonaticides. This same myth also shapes the language used to describe the phenomenon. The most commonly used term, pregnancy denial, assumes that women are aware that they are pregnant and simply unwilling or unable to acknowledge that reality. Yet women's experiences of coming to recognize pregnancy show it to be a complex process as opposed to a binary, with multiple stages that are impacted by numerous individual factors.[34] Researchers who focus on women's perceptions of fertility and recognition of pregnancy note that ambiguity is often present and that these ambiguities are meaningful and useful to women and thus demand greater cultural sensitivity.[35] While the underlying mechanisms driving unperceived pregnancy are still being investigated, it is not a rare occurrence. Unperceived pregnancy after the twentieth week of gestation is more common than triplets, with one case per 300 to 500 pregnancies across Europe and the United States.[36] It may arise from a woman's specific circumstances in which a pregnancy is either unwanted or impossible. Trauma and abuse are present in some cases, but not the majority. Perplexingly, a number of documented cases have appeared without any specific social motivation or psychological illness.

Neuroscientist Natalia Chechko, brain and behavior expert Elena Losse, and psychiatrist Susanne Nehls, a research team that has generated groundbreaking research on unperceived pregnancy, observe that instances of pregnancy denial and subsequent neonaticides that are caused by trauma, such as rape and incest, have long been "under the spotlight," but that such cases are rare. In contrast to common assumptions that unperceived pregnancy arises from a woman's experience of abuse or mental illness, histories of trauma are either "not reported at all or are present only minimally" in documented cases; it is not associated with mental or physiological problems and can thus be experienced by women who are "otherwise healthy." While long-standing stereotypes have overdetermined how these cases are represented and understood, risk is, disturbingly, more widespread; an unrecognized pregnancy is a possibility for any woman under certain circumstances.[37]

Nurse practitioners Doris Vallone and Lori Hoffman open their important 2003 article in *Holistic Nursing Practice* with one such case: a "high achiever" seventeen-year-old patient who was discovered by her mother "dazed," trying to "pull out an umbilical cord," with "blood everywhere" and a newborn baby "still in the toilet."[38] The mother called 911. Everyone survived. The story never made the news. Despite not having perceived her pregnancy, the ambitious, successful high school student was not the victim of abuse or rape and had no prior mental health history. Perhaps her desire to conform to the social and cultural norms of her high school or her perfectionism made embracing the reality of her pregnancy difficult, or perhaps the lack of recognition was purely biological. If her mother had not arrived home in time, the baby could easily have been a neonaticide victim. Echoing Resnick's observance of stigma among health care workers around such cases and call for empathy, Vallone and Hoffman share this teenager's story to undercut nurses' stereotypes about monster moms, which they worry lead to indifferent and even cruel treatment.

Writing for *Military Medicine*, Captain Paige Neifert describes a similar case of unperceived pregnancy that nearly ended in neonaticide. Neifert recounts clinical interviews with a patient she calls Ms. T: a twenty-year-old, active-duty Air Force medical technician who ended one romantic relationship and began a new one in 1999. She used condoms for birth control with both partners and did not consider the possibility that she might have become pregnant prior to the breakup. Despite eventually observing some odd sensations in her abdomen, she did not experience many of what are assumed to be decisive signs of pregnancy: She did not gain sufficient weight to require new clothes, she was never queasy, and she spotted in a way that mimicked menstruation.[39] She enjoyed a close relationship with her parents, who were still married. She had no history of substance abuse, physical abuse, or sexual abuse. Her medical and psychiatric histories as explored in clinical interviews were unremarkable, with no evidence of psychotic, affective, or anxiety disorder. Instead, Ms. T was described as enjoying normal cognitive function, with a certain "unworldly" or winsome manner.

Neifert details how Ms. T's unperceived pregnancy thrust her into a childbirth crisis. While at work on an inpatient ward, Ms. T began to experience severe cramping. She slipped into an empty patient room to rest and was overcome by the symptoms of childbirth. "Too incapacitated by pain to obtain help," she delivered a living, seven-and-a-half-pound baby boy. Confused and in shock, Ms. T left the newborn on the hospital bed still attached to the placenta, stumbled to a bathroom, and was attempting to clean herself when a nurse coincidentally entered the room and discovered the baby struggling to breathe, its body a purplish blue. The nurse immediately began chest compressions. A respiratory therapist on site was able to administer positive-pressure ventilation for several minutes while the baby was stimulated and warmed. His color and breath improved and he was taken to the neonatal intensive care unit for observation.

During clinical interviews after the crisis, Ms. T initially denied any knowledge of having been pregnant. In a follow-up interview, she explained that a month before the birth she had felt what she thought was fetal movement and suspected she might be in the early months of a pregnancy—but certainly not near delivery. "With the abrupt onset of active labor," explains Neifert, "she became overwhelmed and too frightened to call for help. After the unassisted delivery, she thought the neonate was dead because she never heard him cry. This terrified her even more."[40] Despite her demonstrable normalcy, Ms. T came within seconds of accidentally allowing her infant son to die at birth.

Neifert argues that the military's mobilization of numerous clinical and social supports facilitated a positive outcome in Ms. T's case. Not only had Ms. T embraced her son, who was thriving at eighteen months when Neifert's study concluded, but she had also found acceptance in her community: "Ms. T has since married her boyfriend, who has adopted her son. Her parents, although understandably surprised to have a new grandson, have been extremely supportive and accepting of the patient and her child."[41]

Ms. T presents perhaps the single most important case study on unperceived pregnancy and near neonaticide. Her lack of recognition appears to have been incited by naivete, subtle relationship dynamics, and a whiff of magical thinking as opposed to severe mental health problems or abuse. Her pain and terror during the labor rendered her incapable of providing, or even requesting, the medical care her newborn needed to survive. If she had not been at work in a hospital and a nurse had not intervened, her son would have suffocated. The trauma of surviving an unassisted labor leaves women like Ms. T—and like Emile, as we will discuss in the next chapter—in no position to quickly or effectively protect the precarious lives of their newborns. The medical reality of birth alone underscores that it is unrealistic to expect these women to perform with more maternal grace under these conditions.

As evidence of psychological, social, cultural, and now biological factors contributing to infanticide accumulates, questions about how to understand women's agency and thus culpability, or lack thereof, become increasingly difficult to answer. To further explore these questions in Part II, I narrate Addison and Emile's neonaticide case and its adjudication. By virtue of the extensive materials archived in their police file, Addison and Emile's case offers a rare opportunity to observe the interpersonal politics and local legal norms that appear in tragedies like theirs but are typically invisible to journalists and researchers.

At this point, I would be remiss not to reflect on my positionality and its effect on the story that follows, and not to reveal my mixed emotions about publishing this account of Emile's case. I began thinking about the subject of this book a year after I completed my PhD in American studies. As researchers, we are trained to look for gaps and omissions. Despite having completed extensive coursework on American social, cultural, and women's history, I did not come across the subjects of infant abandonment and homicide until I was preparing to teach a course on the history of crime and control in the United States and read Jeffrey Adler's book on violence in nineteenth-century Chicago.[42] I was stunned by his assessment that these were common occurrences that had simply been overlooked, or deemed insignificant, by other historians. I then reviewed the existing research on the topic and confirmed that the subject had largely been ignored outside of forensic psychiatry and law.

During this early stage in my inquiry, I became pregnant with my first child and chose to deliver him in Brooklyn, New York's only freestanding midwife facility, where I had no access to any kind of pain medication (I was not even offered Tylenol after the delivery). The experience was traumatic. I felt death's presence in the room. I recall, more vividly than I would like to, a few hours after the birth, leaning against a hallway wall, dragging myself into a shower, and watching from outside the bounds of my physical body in tearful shock as I bled down the drain. My baby, thankfully, was safe in his father's arms. If I had been unassisted, my baby and I would not have survived. Nine years later, I found myself having a panic attack on my way to my first prenatal checkup for my second child and was diagnosed with pregnancy-triggered post-traumatic stress disorder (PTSD). This personal experience shaped my interest in researching neonaticide because it made me keenly aware of how the medical risk and often traumatic experience of childbirth are rarely mentioned in the literature as meaningful factors in these tragedies. I entered the field wondering how including a detailed account of birth might change the nature of how neonaticide is understood.

My pregnancy-triggered PTSD has been both a source of personal empathy for the women involved in these cases and an obstacle to my inquiry's progress. Interviewing Emile in prison for twelve hours over the course of three days, in addition to reviewing hundreds of crime scene photographs of Addison's corpse, produced physical effects: by the end of my time in Ohio, the skin of my face was inflamed with rosacea and my appetite was gone. During the first two years of the COVID-19 pandemic, I arrived at a stage in the writing process where I needed to reread all of my notes as well as my annotated copy of the transcript from Emile's trial and could not do so for over a year. Oberman, who has become an important mentor of mine over my years of research, describes a similar experience of secondary trauma from her work, noting that her prison interviews gave her insomnia. Our experiences suggest that the research methods needed to more fully understand these tragedies will come at an emotional cost to those willing to bear witness. I also share with Oberman one of the benefits of such work: a heightened awareness of my privileged position in society and the basic resources to which I have access that buoy my parenting.

Sharing this aspect of my personal experience is risky; similar disclosures have been used to discredit other female researchers. The prosecutor in Emile's case rejected the expert testimony of reproductive mental health researcher Dr. Diana Barnes because she has written publicly on her experience with postpartum depression, as if one personal essay negated the scientific rigor of her refereed publications. Rather than invalidating my inquiry, however, my personal experience informs my ability to understand the physical realities of unmedicated childbirth and incorporate them into a scholarly understanding of the moments of crisis and physical and mental trauma, like the one at the center of Emile's case, that culminate in infant death.

PART II

A Double Tragedy

Part II is the culmination of six years of research into the history of neonaticide in the United States and the hidden backstory behind Emile and Addison's tragedy. To prepare, I began by conducting a systematic review of the research literature with every publication in PubMed and ProQuest Central with the subject term(s) infant homicide, infanticide, and/or neonaticide and writing a critical meta-analysis, which was presented at the Society for the Study of Social Problem's national conference.[1] I then used LexisNexis Academic to identify potential case studies, including Emile Weaver's, and requested the transcript of her trial from the Zanesville Municipal Courthouse's clerk. Reading the 700-plus-page transcript of Emile's trial and reviewing her case docket convinced me that her case had sociological value and warranted public scrutiny.

At this early stage in the research process, I reached out to Emile's post-conviction appeals attorney at the Ohio Office of the Public Defender. We decided to conduct an initial hour-long phone interview with Emile, with her post-conviction appeals attorney present, after which I wrote an affidavit on Emile's behalf, with guidance from Michelle Oberman.[2] After the initial interview, I was granted access to documents that have never been reviewed by researchers in this area. The final case study draws on twelve hours of semi-structured interviews with Emile that were conducted privately in person over three consecutive days in the Dayton Correctional Institution in 2017; semi-structured personal interviews with her mother, a childhood friend and two college friends, and a Delta sister; systematic news media analysis of local and national journalism on her case; and personal observations of all relevant sites, including Addison's grave, Emile's hometown, the Muskingum University campus, and the Zanesville Municipal courthouse. In addition, I visited the Ohio Office of the Public Defender in Columbus to review Emile's police file, which includes all discovery materials, interviews with each of the sorority sisters involved, crime scene photographs, the autopsy report, Emile's pretrial psychological evaluation and medical records, text messages and personal letters, and a video recording of Emile's second pre-arrest police interrogation

In Part II, the narrative is constructed with evidence drawn directly from these sources. All of the college students' names have been replaced with pseudonyms. The descriptive details for New Concord, Ohio and Zanesville, Ohio were gathered during my fieldwork in 2017. Things may have changed since then, but this description takes readers back in time to the campus and courthouse as Emile saw them. In chapter 3, all statements in quotation marks are direct quotes. Italicized statements indicate inner monologue as it was reiterated to me during interviews and recorded verbatim or as excerpted from text messages that are included in Emile's police file. In chapter 4, I detail Emile's trial by quoting extensively from the transcript. All dialogue in quotation marks and formatted as script is quoted verbatim from the transcript. In selecting excerpts to include, I aimed to give readers a representative overview of the trial as a whole while emphasizing the numerous echoes between Emile's trial and the historical cases included in Part I. I chose to include almost all of Emile's testimony uninterrupted because it is historically significant—it is rare and risky for a woman who is accused of neonaticide to testify on her own behalf.

In chapters 3 and 4, I refrain from inputting my own analysis and interpretation so that readers can be immersed in the tragedy and trial and discern the many historical throughlines independently. In chapter 5, I follow up by making these throughlines explicit and by putting forward my interpretation of the tragedy, trial, and its implications for future law and policy.

CHAPTER 3

Losing Addison

New Concord, Ohio's largest constituency lives on the campus of Muskingum University. The school's 1,300 undergraduates make up well over half of the town's total population. The tight-knit commuter community boasts seven churches, one hipster café, two quaint historic houses, and a wind turbine. In 2008, John McCain and Sarah Palin stopped in New Concord at the seasonally open Dairy Duchess on their Straight Talk Express bus tour. Like many small American liberal arts colleges, Muskingum has nimbly reinvented itself to keep its doors open. The university's sagging graduation rate of 55 percent, typical of peer institutions, means that at any given time, almost half the student population is on its way to dropping out. In 2009, the school changed its name from Muskingum College to Muskingum University to showcase its graduate and continuing education programs. In glossy aerial photographs on the college's website, Muskingum presents an appealing parklike campus with impressive new amenities.

From above, the campus's wildly varied architectural styles, dating back to its establishment in 1837, are masked by ubiquitous terracotta roofs. A small river winds like a ribbon behind well-manicured sports fields. A modern library, with the vibe of an upscale hotel, offers students sunlit study nooks, upholstered chairs surrounding a wide electric fireplace lined with rounded stones. A new $10 million performance center designed by an architecture firm in Boston offers practice spaces for chamber music. These new amenities point to a larger trend in college expenditures, built to attract a fresh cohort of international students who are deemed ineligible for financial aid.

Across the quad from these posh facilities, older buildings house traditional academic departments. Even these less welcoming institutional spaces celebrate student and alumni success. Fluorescent-lit hallways with aging drop tile ceilings feature optimistic profiles of smiling alumni explaining how delighted they are to be working in economics, history, nursing, and education. As one recent graduate who entered Muskingum at a fourth-grade reading level explained, the school's impressively low student-to-faculty ratio of fourteen to one and free tutoring programs enabled her to graduate on time with a bachelor's degree in criminal justice and write her own senior seminar paper. She doesn't begrudge the university her $60,000 debt.

Addison was born on Lakeside Drive, otherwise known as Greek Row, in the Delta sorority house, up a short hill from the main quad. Neither highly esteemed nor notorious among Muskingum's five sororities, the Delta house is a boxy two-story cape with horizontal white vinyl siding on its first floor that abruptly changes to vertical green wooden shingles up to the roof. A few doors down, other sorority houses peek demurely from behind gumdrop-shaped shrubs and carefully pruned ornamental trees. Lacelike ivy climbs their brick chimneys, with big barn stars and inviting porch swings that match freshly painted trim. The Delta house, in contrast, looks unkempt. But the house has a perfect view of the football field and is a mere one-minute stroll from the student wellness center.

Emile chose Muskingum not for its academics or athletics, but because it felt like, and was relatively close to, home. She followed her friends to the university, to Delta, and to her major (first chemistry, then biology) and her career plans (physician's assistant), both of which her roommate, Jessie, had already decided to pursue.

Emile moved into the Delta house as a sophomore, a year after the university had temporarily evicted the sorority for hazing. Emile and another member of her pledge class that I interviewed told me they were disappointed that they were not hazed: "It would have been fun."[1]

To many on campus, Emile seemed to live a charmed life. Trim, with long blonde hair, she was pretty in a classic girl-next-door way. She'd graduated seventh in her high school class, attended church camps, and earned membership in the National Honor Society while also playing varsity softball and basketball. She arrived on campus in her own new black Dodge Dart, which many of the Deltas would later enjoy borrowing. The car was a rare splurge purchased with her inheritance from her father, who died when she was eleven. Few were aware that she struggled to pay for food that year.

Like many of her peers on campus, Emile was eager to be seen on social media participating in so-called cow life, the students' playful term for a lifestyle of lazing rather than facing tedious adult obligations: tanning, taking midday naps, sending evil text messages, eating fast food, binge drinking, and hooking up as if procreation and STDs were purely hypothetical. But she still thought of herself as a good girl. A laid-back, nonjudgmental presence, Emile was the chosen confidant, stabilizing force, and wingman of many of the Deltas. In every snapshot taken during her first and second years of college, Emile flashes the same toothy grin, matched by intensely smiling clear blue eyes—the same expression she has in all of the middle and high school pictures that crowd her grandparents' mantel. During our interview, her grandfather recalled a cherished memory of taking Emile out for her first practice date when she was eight years old. The pair dressed up and went out for a nice dinner, an event designed to show Emile how a proper date should transpire. Despite the events of her sophomore year, Emile's ability to appear appropriately happy never wavered.

In the fall of her sophomore year, Emile decided to go on birth control for the first time. Another undergraduate on campus was attending her classes visibly pregnant. Her changing body, especially her large size, attracted daily negative comments that caught Emile's attention. Emile felt hints of stomach pains, but she quickly dismissed these sensations because both she and her mother experienced a similar kind of abdominal discomfort chronically and because she was not gaining weight noticeably, like her pregnant peer. The contrast was reassuring. The gossip, however, was a reminder that being pregnant was not a viable option unless she was ready to simultaneously be the center of attention and an outcast.

When she went to the student wellness center to pick up her prescription, she was shocked to be required to take a pregnancy test first. She skipped her second appointment at the center, at which the results would have been discussed. When the center called to follow up, Emile did not pick up the call. After three emails and three unreturned messages, the center mailed Emile a certified letter with the news. Emile signed for the letter but claimed later, under oath, that she never opened it, though she forced herself to raise her concerns about the test results to her ex-boyfriend, Brian A, a star baseball player from a well-off conservative Christian family in Cincinnati. He and Emile had met at a bonfire party during freshmen orientation. Emile's first love from home, an on-again-off-again high school sweetheart, had been a Brian; meeting this new

Brian so soon into college felt like a nudge from fate to date him. Yet mutual friends found the couple's emotional style draining; they stayed attached to each other through multiple breakups, even when Brian A trashed Emile's room and barked degrading obscenities at her. Brian A didn't return for a second year at Muskingum, but the couple stayed in touch by text message, where Emile raised her pregnancy concerns as a timid sidenote to their exchange of homemade pornography.

Emile hoped Brian A would be supportive about the possible pregnancy. Instead he demanded secrecy—"No one needs to know. You aren't pregnant anyway. Send the pictures you promised. If your roommate is home, go in the bathroom"[2]—though he agreed to drive with her to an appointment at Planned Parenthood an hour away. At this appointment, Emile would take a pregnancy test and review the results and possible options, including safe surrender, adoption, and abortion, with a counselor. Ohio law would then require her to reflect on her decision for twenty-four hours before making a second appointment. On the day of the appointment, a rare ice storm made the roads impassable. The couple was forced to turn back. Claiming he was busy with baseball, Brian A refused to escort Emile to another appointment.

After the failed attempt to reach Planned Parenthood, Emile began to repeat a mantra to herself: *It will go away. This isn't really happening to me.* There was no baby and no need for an abortion. She monitored herself for decisive signs of pregnancy but found only ambiguity; she still had not gained a dramatic amount of weight nor experienced the nausea of morning sickness; she wasn't exactly menstruating, but she did observe spotting.

In this muddled state of knowing and not knowing, Emile continued to conform to the established habits of campus life as she had the year before, attending classes and frat parties on ritualistic autopilot. Emile's daily interactions confirmed her approach: Throughout the winter, none of her sorority sisters, classmates, professors, or Greek Life advisors said anything to her about the pregnancy. Emile made a few self-conscious jokes about her weight gain but continued to change clothes in front of her roommate and closest friend in the Delta house, Jessie, until late in the spring term. Like any good best friend, Jessie proactively defended Emile's reputation by shooting down rumors circulating on her cheerleading squad.

Less than a month before Addison's birth, Emile changed into formal wear for a cousin's wedding in front of her mother and stepfather, making no effort to hide her body from them. Both adults saw her stripped down to just a sports bra and underpants and, aside from her minor weight gain, which seemed healthy, noticed nothing different about her.

A week later, Emile's high school sweetheart, Brian B, happened to be out partying with friends in New Concord. At the end of a long night, he made his way to Emile's room to sleep. In the morning, she nonchalantly changed in front of him. He either didn't notice or chose not to comment on her pregnancy.

One of Emile's Delta sisters spoke later about drawing Emile into a firm hug around this time to figure out if her suspicions were correct. Once she was able to feel Emile's stomach pressed against her own, rock hard and round like a basketball, she knew that Emile was pregnant. Summer break was a couple weeks away. She assumed Emile would go home after classes ended and have the baby. She wasn't concerned for Emile's or the baby's safety, nor was she surprised that Emile would hide an unplanned, out-of-wedlock pregnancy with an ex who was already busy exchanging flirty texts with another Delta sister. It would be impossible to recover from the malicious gossip that would follow such an admission. It felt polite to not force the issue.

One might wonder, at this point, why the Deltas did not organize an intervention or call a counselor. Yet even many doctors and mental health professionals are poorly informed on unperceived pregnancy and its relationship to neonaticide risk. While one might wish that the Deltas had taken action to help Emile, it is not a fair expectation when the realities of how denial works are factored in. Denial is a commonly relied upon coping mechanism and one that is known to be socially co-constructed. Research finds that women who deny their pregnancies tend to be successful at convincing those nearest to them, including parents and even sexual partners, that they are not pregnant.[3] Being a good friend often involves humoring a friend's better story for themselves.

By Greek Week in April, Emile was nine months pregnant. She was also expected to play in a sorority dodgeball tournament that she had helped the Deltas win the previous year. The week before the game, the Deltas noticed that Emile had started to wear bulky sweat suits and carry a stuffed animal or laptop over her midsection. She was also seen taking black cohosh, an herbal supplement that is wrongly thought to induce miscarriage. Despite these ambiguous signs of apprehension, Emile showed up for the dodgeball game in the team's snug T-shirt and shorts—an outfit tighter than anything she had worn in public in several weeks. In the frenzied mass of lobbed rubber balls and sprinting young women, Emile stood out, athletic as ever, her rounded belly visible but not obtrusive. But caught off guard by a particularly hard hit, she fell hip first against the unyielding floor. Spectators gasped.

The dodgeball game intensified rumors on campus. Emile's closest college friend, Aden, noticed what appeared to be a growing baby bump and pulled Emile aside during a weekend trip to a mall in Columbus to ask if she was pregnant. She said no. He didn't believe her but declined to question her further, assuming her roommate would eventually step in to handle the situation.

A few days later, Delta house manager and close friend Charlotte approached Emile in the house's kitchen and asked if she was pregnant. With several other Delta sisters looking on, Emile flatly rejected the question with a matter-of-fact no, then continued boiling herself a hot dog. The matter seemed settled.

Less than a week later, Emile woke up in the middle of the night in intense stomach pain. Her abdominal muscles strained uncontrollably. She rushed downstairs to the Delta house's smallest and most private restroom, referred to as the study bathroom, just in time to release her bowels. For the next six hours, she weathered what felt to her like the stomach flu that had plagued many of her sorority sisters the week before. She pooped a lot, in waves, then rested. The bathroom was small enough for her to sit on the toilet and, leaning forward, rest her steaming forehead against the cool tile sink.

When the labor intensified, Emile lost consciousness. Her dead weight snapped the top of the toilet seat off its fixture. When she regained consciousness, she was overcome by the unbearable pressure of the baby crowning. She forced herself to feel between her legs, which somehow felt like they belonged to someone else. Something hard, about the size of an avocado, was pressing through her labia. She could feel wetness and thin strands of human hair. She'd never experienced a miscarriage, but this, she thought, is what it must feel like.

Fresh blood stained her hands and thighs. Cloudy, strong-smelling fluid puddled at her feet. Panicked and immobilized, she reached between her legs and wrapped the tips of her fingers around the top of the protruding skull. She pulled down. The bulk and heft of the nearly seven-pound newborn ripped through multiple three-inch-deep vaginal lacerations directly into the toilet bowl. Numb, gutted, and completely alone, Emile found herself squatting above a mass of tissue and organs.

Emile first tried to flush the toilet, then, as it overflowed, she reached into the bowl and lifted everything out. She laid the baby on the floor next to the placenta. With her blood-soaked gym shorts tucked between her legs, she ventured the short distance from the study bathroom to the kitchen. She took an unused trash bag out of the kitchen garbage can and selected a clean steak knife. She carried both back to the bathroom and sat next to the throbbing, intricately veined placenta on the tile floor. Early morning light began to drift into the Delta house through dusty metal blinds. Soon the Deltas would come down for breakfast.

Without feeling, Emile focused on cleaning up. She didn't want to leave a mess or acknowledge the miscarriage: *It will heal*, she told herself. *It will go away.*[4] She cut the umbilical cord and looked at the tiny body on the floor, seemingly only six inches long. It appeared lifeless. Frantic, she began to swipe at all the blood on the floor and walls with paper towels. Her gym shorts were saturated with blood and fluid; she threw them into the garbage bag, then added the placenta, then the baby.

Consciousness waning, desperately thirsty, and disoriented, Emile felt blood streaming down her legs. Oddly pungent sweat glazed her skin. She tied the bag loosely, then lifted it by the knot. She could have walked down the driveway and placed the bag inside one of the cans waiting for that morning's trash pickup, but part of her felt that it deserved a burial.[5] She left the garbage bag in the driveway next to the kitchen door and dragged herself back into the house. Unable to walk up the flight of stairs to her bedroom, she lay down on the couch in the library, in front of the study bathroom. She was still lying there—bleeding, sweating, too calm—as the Deltas with morning classes came down for breakfast. Despite her effort to clean up, the bathroom still looked like the set of a Quentin Tarantino movie.

When several Deltas alerted Charlotte about the state of the study bathroom, her professionalism snapped then rebounded. She found the seat from the toilet resting askew on the bowl. Syrupy pink fluid pooled around the base of the toilet and sink. Blood speckled with bits of tissue stained the floor. The trash bag had been removed from the can, which was overturned. A bloodstained steak knife rested in plain sight on a shelf above the mess. Worse, the tiny airless room had a distinct, foreboding stench. Charlotte didn't recognize the pong of childbirth, but the musk and stress of the human body's most extreme act lingered. Instead of getting a mop, Charlotte reached for her cell phone: "Whoever made the mess in the study bathroom needs to clean it up ASAP," she texted the Delta sisters. "It looks like a murder scene. Also, it is unsanitary and disgusting. You need to clean it up ASAP. Or if there's a problem and you need to talk about it, I am here and I can help you."[6] Emile, self-exiled from the group chat, would not have seen Charlotte's message even if she had been well enough to pick up her phone.

On their way to class, several Deltas walked past Emile curled up on the couch in the library in front of the study bathroom. Her long wavy blond hair was plastered with sweat against her skull. Her pupils were dilated. Her pale skin, now nearly translucent, had a chalky quality. Dangerously dehydrated, she appeared to be a mere indentation on the couch. But she told the Delta sisters who passed her that she had spent the night on the toilet with the same rough stomach flu that others had weathered a week earlier. In shock, she was only vaguely aware of bleeding heavily. *It will heal; it will go away*, she recalls wishing, the mantra silencing the din of her pressing medical emergency.[7]

Emile eventually made her way to her bed upstairs and fell asleep there. At five P.M., she and Jessie drove to McDonald's, where Emile consumed two cheeseburgers, fries, and a large iced sweet tea. Both Emile and Jessie were surprised by her appetite. Jessie was also surprised that Emile's stomach appeared flatter than the day before, even after the feast.

A little after seven P.M., Emile took a brief break from studying to text Brian A.

no more baby

what, Brian A replied.

no more baby

how do you know?

taken care of

how????

don't worry about it

why won't you tell me?

you haven't cared this whole time. I really don't feel like talking about it.

abortion? I'd like to know how you killed my kid

fuck off, Brian

damn, why didn't you just tell me

why do you care now?

just wondering

I went into labor last night for six hours. It was a girl with your dark hair. But didn't make it due to placenta complications

holy shit, I'm sorry, and what is that, and does everyone know?

no one knows, went by myself.[8]

At eight P.M., Deltas Whitney, Megan, and Sammy were driving home from a debate team competition and discussing Charlotte's text message. Amid rising suspicion, they picked up Emile's roommate and went out for ice cream at the Dairy Duchess. They invited Emile to join them, but she declined. In her absence, they considered—not for the first time—the possibility that Emile was pregnant. Increasingly agitated, the sisters resolved to contact a counselor in the morning. In the meantime, given the state of the study bathroom, Whitney wondered out loud if Emile might have already "thrown it away."[9]

When the four sisters arrived back at the house, they decided to investigate. Earlier, several Deltas had observed a glitch in their highly micromanaged house cleaning routine: The bag from the kitchen garbage can was full and resting on the ground in the driveway next to the house, rather than in the trash cans at the end of the driveway. While Jessie and Sammy waited in the car, Whitney and Megan decided to lift, then shake the bag. Dangling it curiously above the tarmac, they felt an alarming weight. They tried to untie the knot at the top of the bag, but it held fast.

The pale light seeping through the Delta house's kitchen windows out onto the driveway only heightened the darkness of the spring night engulfing them. Whitney and Megan turned on a cell phone flashlight, then ripped a hole in the side of the bag. A baby's tiny foot and leg became visible, then her eyes and hair. It was a newborn tossed among blood-soaked paper towels and a used Polar Pop cup.

Both women fled back to the car. Then Megan returned to the garbage bag to confirm the unthinkable. She doubled over, nauseated. All four girls, fearing that Emile would see them from her bedroom window, piled into the car and drove off. Emile didn't notice the sisters retching in the driveway. She was too busy preparing a presentation, due the next day, for her history seminar on women in the Middle Ages.

While continuing to cry and panic and with no clear protocol on how to manage this kind of crisis, the sorority sisters drove to a nearby secluded parking lot. Their first phone call was not to the police, or to 911, or to the campus wellness center, or to Emile's mother. Instead, the girls chose a confidant closer to their inner circle: their house's Greek Life advisor, Amy Archer. Amy, in turn, called Stacey Allen, the head of Greek Life for the university.

Stacey contacted Susan Waryck, the associate dean of student life, who was the first to call the campus police. It is unclear exactly how much time elapsed between the initial discovery of the dead baby and the first call to the authorities. It is also unclear what the sisters and their Greek Life advisor were occupied with before they secured emergency assistance. Three layers of the university's administration were aware of the discovery before any move was made to check the baby's vital signs—or Emile's.

Responding to Susan's call, Patrolman Mark Stelzer of the Muskingum University Police Department arrived at the Delta house a little after nine P.M. He found a ripped trash bag in the driveway that matched the sisters' description. After discovering the dead baby swaddled in dried blood and garbage, he rushed to contact the Muskingum County's Sheriff's Department.

When additional officers arrived at the Delta house, the sisters were instructed to leave their cell phones on a coffee table and assemble outside. Cautiously the sisters stepped out into the spring night. If they had been allowed to chat, it might have felt like an impromptu fire drill, but they were not. Instead they were arranged in evenly distributed rows and instructed to stand silently as Patrolman Stelzer, now joined by Officer Mindy Peck, established a security zone around the perimeter of their house with yellow plastic caution tape.

Several detectives huddled in the driveway over the dead newborn, waiting for the crime scene photographer to arrive. It must have been difficult for the officers with children to leave the newborn splayed on the asphalt. Despite being rigid and cold to the touch, Addison still possessed the sweetness of any infant. She was curled loosely on her side in a natural fetal position. She had not been cleaned by a nurse or midwife, so the cheeks of her bottom were still fastened together with black meconium. The vernix, a creamy, white, glue-like substance that protects the softness of a newborn's skin, had dried and started to peel away. Stripes of blood and bright red tissue tie-dyed her back and neck. Through the gore, however, her skin held a pink petal tone. Her cherubic lips gaped open, as if she were trying to inhale. Even though she was dead and lying on a garbage bag, she looked as if she could have been rocking peacefully in a bassinet, wrapped in a lambskin.

While police secured the crime scene and began interviewing the sorority sisters in their patrol cars, medics Alan Graham and Shane Barkley entered the Delta house. They walked past bedrooms overstuffed with teenage memorabilia, unmade beds loaded with stuffed animals and laundry, plastic bins filled with makeup and body products. Fuzzy animal-foot slippers stood guard alongside zebra-striped galoshes and party heels. Wall space was shellacked with aphorisms: "Be Your Own Beautiful!" "If You Think I Am Crazy, Meet My BIG" (sorority speak for assigned big sister), "Whitney and Sammy Twerk Camp."[10]

Alan and Shane climbed the stairs to the second floor and found Emile perched calmly on her pink-and-white striped sheets, talking with Susan Waryck. When they entered the bedroom, Susan was asking Emile about her classes for the year ahead. Emile had just explained that she was planning on taking three biology courses, including anatomy, which Susan advised might be too challenging of a course load.

When asked directly by Alan and Shane if she was okay, Emile's answer was a polite but emphatic yes. The medics noted that her collected demeanor was undercut by a palpable anxiety and dilated pupils. But they did not press her for more information or encourage her to seek medical care. Instead, Emile was escorted to the campus police station without the support of her family or the expertise of a lawyer.

By 10:30 P.M., Emile was alone with Detective Todd Mahle, a twenty-one-year veteran of the force. Mahle had investigated a nearly identical tragedy twelve years earlier, at a campus residence less than a block away from Emile's sorority house: A twenty-two-year-old junior had given birth into a toilet, alone, and placed the newborn boy into a garbage bag, where he died of suffocation several minutes later. By the time Detective Mahle was driving to campus to interrogate Emile, local newspapers were already typesetting headlines announcing: "Dead Baby is Second at University Since 2002."

When Detective Mahle arrived at the university's police station to interview Emile, he was surprised: small, shabby, with two shades of mud brown paint, the station looked, to Detective Mahle, just like a two-story house. He had conducted the junior's interrogations in his own station. Campus police sent the detective to the break/training room, where Emile, who had changed into red Ohio State sweatpants and a bulky hooded sweatshirt, was watching a basketball game. She had voluntarily relinquished her cell phone and wallet to the police and made no request for legal counsel; she did not attempt to leave the station, even after Detective Mahle told her that she was not under arrest and was therefore free to do so. When Detective Mahle asked if she needed anything, she declined. Despite having eaten only once since the birth, and without having spoken to her family or receiving any medical care, Emile remained alert and polite. The weight of her pelvic bones pressing into the plastic chair must have burned due to her severe vaginal injuries, but she doesn't recall feeling anything other than noticeably numb.

Emile's first halting confessions, offered between 10:30 P.M. and 3:40 A.M. less than twenty-four hours after the birth, were recorded in four pages of Detective Mahle's handwritten notes, which later became an exhibit in the state's trial against her.[11]

Detective Mahle began with a simple question: "Do you know why you are here?"

"The fire department told me I was okay," Emile replied.

Detective Mahle then sat next to Emile and looked directly at her. "Did you have a baby?"

"No."

"Listen," Detective Mahle said. "You're twenty years old; you're a college student; you must realize that we can figure out if you've had a baby by blood and DNA."

The forensic evidence was months away from being analyzed, but Emile capitulated: "Yes," she had just given birth.

Without prompting, according to Mahle's notes, Emile then told him about her pregnancy: "She [Emile] really wasn't that big. Things started feeling funny. She never took a test. She always felt heavy pains in her stomach [even before the pregnancy]. She didn't want to say anything, didn't want anyone to know."

When asked why she had put the baby in the trash bag, she said that she "didn't know what else to do with it. It wasn't making any noise." She had tried to "clean up."

When asked if anyone else knew she was pregnant, Emile said that "there were rumors around campus." But she hadn't felt nauseous or experienced any of the other typical signs of pregnancy.

Detective Mahle's notes contain no information about the birth itself, beyond the eventual positioning of the newborn in the toilet. He either did not ask or did not feel it was relevant to record any other details about the labor. He also failed to note that Emile was bleeding during the interview. She had arrived at the station without any menstrual products, so had stuffed her underwear and vagina with the few napkins and paper towels she could find in the station's kitchenette.

Pressed repeatedly by Mahle, she eventually speculated that the baby may have breathed shallowly for a few minutes and perhaps moved an ankle. But, she told the detective, the baby was only six inches long and appeared dead. "It wasn't making any noise," she explained. "I put it outside and then cleaned everything up. I didn't know what to do. I didn't know if I should bury it. I should have gone to the hospital."

When asked if she had choked the baby intentionally, Emile said no: "There's no way I could even comprehend something like that." "Did you want the baby to live?" the detective asked. His notes say she responded, "I was more concerned about my safety. I didn't want the baby to die. I don't want this to seem like I intentionally killed the kid."

Mahle noted that Emile's demeanor struck him as oddly unemotional. "She was never disrespectful," he recalls. "She was alert and polite, and most of the time quick to answer, but she just showed no emotion [other than] being tired." At 3:40 A.M., he brought the interview to a close. Emile asked if she could return to the Delta house—she explained that she had to deliver a presentation in the morning for her history class. The detective told her that she had already been put on summary suspension and would not be allowed back into the Delta house. She was already locked out of the campus's online systems and erased from the campus directory. Without her phone or wallet and unable to walk more than a few steps at a time, Emile accepted an offer from the campus police to stay overnight at the station. She was led to a small, windowless room filled with large, locked storage closets, given a throw blanket, and left to lie bleeding on the floor.

The day Emile had gone into labor, her mother, Sandy Potts, who suffers from numerous chronic health problems, had undergone a hysterectomy. The following morning, through the blur of opioid painkillers and lingering anesthesia, Sandy received an alarming Facebook message from one of Emile's sorority sisters. At first Sandy assumed that the message urging her to "start driving to campus NOW. It's an emergency" was a tasteless prank.

Before she could dismiss the first message, however, a second arrived. This one came from Charlotte and also insisted that Sandy rush to campus. Charlotte vaguely warned of a bloody steak knife. Had Emile been stabbed on the campus of her private Presbyterian university? Clouded mind racing, Sandy was grateful that the girls were telling her to drive to campus, not a hospital. Before leaving, she searched online for breaking news about the university, finding only a headline she couldn't understand: "Dead Baby Found on Campus." Once she arrived at the university, she called the campus police station and was told by an officer to drive to the Delta house. There, heavily made-up TV newscasters from the Sinclair Broadcast Group and their crew crowded the sorority house's front lawn, but there was no sign of Emile.

An hour passed. No one from the university met Sandy or called her to explain the situation. Still groggy, she was certain she had been misguided and headed to the campus police station. "It was just one game after another to keep Emile alone," Sandy later insisted.[12]

In the hour that Sandy waited outside the sorority house, Emile had voluntarily undergone a second interrogation, this time on video. Mahle arrived impeccably dressed, in a tan suit and white collared shirt. His military-style haircut was spiked to a crisp. Emile, who had not yet received a meal or medical attention, was wearing the same sweatpants she slept in. She had not been formally charged and had not been read her rights. Unprepared to confide in her mother, she did not request a phone call or ask for a lawyer.

As soon as Sandy entered the campus police station, she recalls being overwhelmed by the smell of Emile's blood. Paper towels and napkins had done little to slow the heavy flow of blood and tissue and Emile's red sweatpants were soaked through. "I just couldn't bring my mind to understand why Emile hadn't been taken to a hospital," Sandy told me later. "Why wasn't she cared for?"[13] Before Sandy and Emile left the station, they were told to expect a murder charge and that Emile should find legal counsel. In the car, Emile sank into the passenger seat, begged for a Tylenol, then fell into a deep lasting sleep. Stunned, her energy waning, Sandy struggled to focus on the road ahead—but despite having been warned about a murder charge, Sandy accepted Emile's explanation that she had miscarried and refrained from asking follow-up questions.

Once Sandy and Emile arrived home, Emile asked for more Tylenol, then immediately retreated to her attic bedroom. Sandy wanted Emile to see a doctor, but, under the impression that Emile had only miscarried, agreed to let her rest while she focused on making arrangements with a lawyer in Columbus. In the middle of the night, Emile woke up urgently needing to pee. Using the walls for support, she tried to walk quietly to the bathroom. Halfway there, struggling with the stab of the urine's acidity, significant blood loss, and raging anemia, she fainted. The sound of Emile's body hitting the floor shocked Sandy awake. She found Emile unable to lift herself from the floor and supported her to the toilet, then back to bed, where she climbed in with her—a small comfort mother and daughter would maintain through the summer.

The next morning, against Emile's wishes, Sandy drove her to one of the nearest emergency rooms that accepted their insurance in West Virginia. The attending physician performed a pelvic ultrasound and revised Emile's diagnosis from bleeding and pain caused by a miscarriage to "unspecified abortion, without mention of complication, incomplete." Performed immediately on an emergency basis, Emile's dilation and curettage (D&C) operation revealed bilateral labia lacerations and a deep tear of Emile's vaginal floor. The doctor noted, "It appears the patient has delivered a term infant recently," and revised her diagnosis to "probable postpartum state."[14] The hospital immediately contacted the Parkersburg Police Department.

In the surgery waiting area, Sandy was joined by Officer Shane Semones. She agreed to answer his questions without legal counsel present, though she lied and told him that Emile had miscarried at home. She also allowed the officer to interview Emile in her hospital bed, alone, where she was still reeling from the effects of the powerful cocktail of medications administered for her surgery. These included propofol, which diminishes consciousness and memory; midazolam, a powerful sedative administered prior to surgery to prevent the formation of new memories and block anxiety; and fentanyl, the single most potent opioid analgesic, or pain reliever. Unsurprisingly, given the effects of these medications, Emile's conversation with Officer Semones introduced new inconsistencies into her previous account of events. She told the officer that she'd had a miscarriage three days prior, and had realized it only after she looked in the toilet and saw a "mass of tissue" that "kind of looked like a baby." She stated that the fetus was "approximately four inches in length" and that she "left the fetus in the toilet and laid down for a couple of hours." She then stated that her roommate had called her mother and Emergency Medical Services, who examined her and told her "she was fine." Notes from this interview were given to Detective Mahle, then to the prosecutor.[15]

After the post-surgery interrogation, Emile refused to leave Sandy's house for anything but trips to the hospital to address issues including the persistent appearance of blood in her urine and stool, anemia, low hemoglobin, bleeding hemorrhoids, and a two-week period of uninterrupted constipation. Eventually diagnosed with major depression and agoraphobia, Emile began to see a grief counselor.

As Emile sank into the aftermath of her unattended childbirth, Addison's corpse was transported to the Licking County Coroner's Office for an autopsy. The full autopsy and toxicology reports were not completed until June, but Addison's death certificate, issued in early May, listed her cause of death as "presumed asphyxiation." Close communication between the Muskingum County Sheriff's Department and the Licking County Coroner's Office ensured that those responsible for scientifically determining the cause of Addison's death were well aware that she had been found inside a garbage bag and thus the "presumed" cause of death was determined prior to any actual forensic work being conducted. As C. Jeff Lee, the chief forensic pathologist in the Licking office, explained in a letter to Charles Feicht, chief forensic pathologist in the Muskingum County Coroner's Office: "According to information given to me, this infant was found in a tied plastic bag sitting on the ground."[16]

After the autopsy was completed, the coroner placed Addison's removed organs in a plastic bag and sewed her whole. Reassembled, Addison was returned to Emile's family for burial.

Despite her desire to disappear into the attic's rafters, Emile responded to the return of Addison's corpse by rallying to the tasks that faced her: naming a newborn daughter and dressing her for an open casket funeral. She chose the name Addison Grace and accompanied Sandy to the nearest Babies "R" Us to select an outfit for Addison to wear in her miniature casket. Among the racks of soft cotton onesies, as she touched each outfit more adorable and more cheerful than the last, Emile felt her lungs constrict. Pearls of sweat patterned her forehead. She selected a buttery yellow pajama set, patterned with ducklings and with a matching beanie big enough to cover the yawning scars around the circumference of Addison's skull. Then she fled to the parking lot in time for a panic attack to rip through every cell in her body.

For the first time, Emile's protective scrim of denial evaporated. Addison was no longer the "it" Emile had imagined her to be, but Emile's beloved daughter. In the busy Babies "R" Us parking lot, Emile cowered in the face of her own culpability; she saw herself as a monster, just as all of the newspaper headlines had described her. In the tumult of self-loathing, her feelings of loss and bereavement multiplied. A new grief consumed her.

At Addison's funeral, surrounded by her siblings and grandparents, Emile was composed, if also vacant. While Sandy's sobs reverberated throughout the brief religious service, Emile kept quiet, dabbing sharply at the corners of her leaking eyes with a tissue like a bird pecking at seeds. After the remarks were over, Sandy approached the casket and lifted Addison to her chest, where she held her for several long moments before reluctantly placing her back in the casket. Other family members led her, overcome by emotion, away from the casket. Emile's grandmother held her fingers to Addison's soft belly, as she had touched her napping children and grandchildren. As she backed away from the casket, she worried that Emile seemed hopeless.

CHAPTER 4

Losing Emile

Bedazzled with baroque-revival elements in the grandiose Second Empire style popular at the start of the twentieth century, the face of the municipal courthouse in Zanesville, Ohio, matches its maximum-sentence reputation. Much like the building's facade, the inside of the main courtroom strains for grandeur but achieves something closer to camp. A floor-to-ceiling portrait of Lady Justice is shellacked to the wall behind the judge's bench, looking like the largest appliqué sticker ever made. The courthouse's only public restrooms must be entered from the outside: the doors read "Men" and "Ladies Lounge."[1]

Emile, on her way to trial, did not have a chance to pause in the Ladies Lounge. She did, however, spend the year ahead of her trial behind the courthouse, in Muskingum County Jail. Charged with gross abuse of a corpse, two counts of tampering with evidence, and aggravated murder—an offense punishable by the death penalty—Emile was taken into the state's custody three months after Addison's death. She had proven herself neither a public safety nor flight risk over the summer, but her bail was still set at $1 million, a sum her mother's disability checks could hardly cover. Emile joined the almost 50,000 inmates held by Ohio. The state runs the sixth-largest prison system in the United States, at a cost of nearly $1.8 billion annually.

Built in 1974, Muskingum County Jail was designed to house fifty inmates. By the time Emile was admitted, it was tasked with holding 180 people, a number far exceeding the state's documented guidelines for cell square footage. To accommodate these numbers, the state opted for an open floor plan over individual cells with bunk beds and exposed showers and toilets in the same warehouse-sized room. Tiah Clark, a nurse at the jail, explains that the biggest challenge with overcrowding is that "nobody has enough room to detox."[2] When a 2014 report flagged the jail's overcrowding issue, Sarah Andrews, then the managing director of Ohio Parole and Community Services, noted that allowing jails to inspect themselves was "probably not a good plan."[3] My requests to tour the facility were denied.

In the numerous handwritten letters Emile exchanged with her sorority sisters during her year in jail, both sides focused squarely on the drama in the Delta house and on campus. In hundreds of pages of spiral-bound notebook paper festooned with drawings of hearts, flowers, and cartoon animals, the sisters talked about their campus crushes while Emile, as a journalist in *Elle* wrote in an article about her case, sounded like she was enjoying a year abroad.[4] She never complained about or even called attention to the experience of confinement, which would have included subsisting on something akin to cat food, witnessing strangers violently detox, and managing her own menstruation-triggered PTSD in overused public toilets and showers.

In the meantime, both sides were preparing their legal teams for Emile's trial. The firm Sandy had originally hired to represent Emile quit a week before the trial, when Emile refused a plea deal that would have required her to admit to having planned and intentionally carried out Addison's murder in exchange for twenty years behind bars. Defense attorney R. Arron Miller stepped in at the last minute. The four Yelp reviews for his now permanently closed law office range from "Amazing!" to "Total waste of time & money." The most in-depth review praises the diligence of Miller's female assistant. Sandy hired Miller because of his quasi-success representing the defendant in the nearly identical case that Detective Todd Mahle had investigated eleven years before on the Muskingum University campus in which, like Emile, a junior concealed her pregnancy, labored alone on a toilet, and, while cleaning up, placed her infant inside a garbage bag. The judge in the earlier case prohibited the use of evidence gathered during Mahle's initial interrogations of the junior; a different judge assigned to Emile's case, Judge Mark Fleegle, did not impose the same restriction during her trial. In the absence of evidence from her initial interrogation, the junior received a three-year sentence and was released early.

Muskingum County Prosecutor Michael Haddox, who would represent the state in Emile's trial, had also prosecuted that student. Reflecting on the case in an interview with *The Columbus Dispatch*, Haddox called the three-year sentence a "real travesty of justice"[5]—a sentiment shared by numerous local newspapers and expressed in editorials at the time. Haddox had known Fleegle since 1985, when both worked in the felony division of the prosecutor's office. In an article in the *Times Recorder*, Haddox reminisced about collaborating with Fleegle "as a team": "I think the first year I came over [to the prosecutor's office], Mark and I tried like twenty-five jury trials between common pleas court and county court. We had a lot of fun and worked well together."[6] When Fleegle left for the bench, Haddox stepped into the elected position of chief prosecutor.

One case that haunts Mahle and Haddox also underscores the role of faith in their sense of their professional purpose. Both men devoted themselves to finding justice for twenty-nine-year-old murder victim Celeste Fronsman. In 2012, Fronsman was severely beaten and burned alive. She was a drug addict and prostitute but the extreme circumstances of her killing generated a great deal of sympathy. It was the first time Mahle and Haddox encountered fourth- and fifth-degree burns deep enough to destroy muscle tissue and reach bone. In that condition, Fronsman managed to drag herself a third of a mile through the woods out onto Interstate 208, where she was found by a driver to whom she managed to articulate the names of her assailants before permanently losing consciousness. Mahle and Haddox marvel at Fronsman's ordeal. For Haddox, the only explanation for Fronsman's actions is "divine intervention." For Mahle: "There are so many things about this case where I think, 'The good Lord was on our side.'"[7]

On Monday, May 16, 2016, Emile's trial began with her sitting alone. None of her family members were present. Members of a conservative church community, her grandparents did not feel it would be appropriate to attend. Her stepfather opted out of publicly supporting her. Sandy attended the trial daily but, having been named as a potential witness, was forced to stay in the hallway, outside of the courtroom's closed doors. She was never called to testify. Several other close friends, including Aden, were also listed as potential witnesses and were thus also locked out. Due to the trauma inflicted by discovering Addison's corpse, the Deltas were legally defined as victims of Emile's crime. This status situated them on the side of the prosecution.

Haddox and his assistant prosecutor, Ron Welch, opened jury selection by asking for a show of hands: "How many people here are nervous right now?" asked Welch. "I see many hands. Okay." Judge Fleegle followed up: "Have any of you formed or expressed an opinion as to the guilt or innocence of the defendant in this case?" All twelve potential jurors raised their hands. Stories about Emile had already reached a global audience, with headlines from Peru to the United Kingdom quoting from her text messages to Brian A: "'No More Baby': Ex-sorority sister charged with murder after dumping newborn in bin." The rest of the day was spent walking through the basic functions of the court and reviewing the nature and origin of each potential juror's existing bias toward Emile, a process intended to dispel the notion that jurors' exposure to media coverage of the case meant they couldn't remain impartial. Several jurors made admissions in closed chambers that led to them being excused. Private during the trial but included in the official transcript, only one such admission was sympathetic toward Emile. While interviewing each juror, Haddox and Welch built rapport by offering comforting analogies between jury duty and more familiar activities, such as working on cars, cooking and baking for grandchildren, and fishing. "What do you like to do with your free time?" Welch asked a potential juror. "Travel and planning a wedding," she replied. "Oh, congratulations. Good for you. And having a wife that planned a wedding, I know that takes a lot of time," Welch commiserated.[8]

Emile's defense attorney, Miller, remained silent during jury selection. Aside from making a few comments during private discussions in the judge's chamber with several jurors who were then excused, Miller did not pose a single follow-up question or make any effort to engage with or vet the potential jurors.

In opening statements the next morning, Haddox spoke at length, and with great feeling. He slowly and systematically walked the jury through the months leading up to and the immediate aftermath of Addison's birth, highlighting key elements of his argument that would repeat in witness testimony. "Despite questions and requests from her very, very best friends," lamented Haddox, Emile "refused to admit that she was pregnant. On the other hand, Weaver had not been acting like she was pregnant." Aside from drinking alcohol and "smoking marijuana," Haddox told the jurors, Emile was taking black cohosh pills, having sex with two different Brians, and playing dodgeball aggressively.

Drawing on the interviews Emile gave to law enforcement immediately after Addison's birth and while sedated after her D&C procedure, Haddox zoomed in on each inconsistency in Emile's story as evidence that she had been intentionally deceitful. She told Detective Mahle that "the baby wasn't making any noise and she didn't know what to do, so she cleaned up everything and set it outside," Haddox informed the jurors. "Then she indicated that she thought the baby may have been breathing and moving, but not that much."

Haddox saved his harshest rebukes for Emile's emotional style. Not only was Emile "unemotional and acting normal" at the time Addison's corpse was discovered, she was "more concerned about her own safety than the baby's" during and immediately after her unassisted labor. At the end of the labor, Haddox noted that Emile "thought she was losing more blood than she should have . . . she tried to stop her own bleeding . . . When asked, she admitted, 'I didn't do anything to keep her alive.' When questioned why, she stated, 'Because I was more concerned about my health . . . I could have washed her face off, but I didn't. I was more concerned about myself." These quotations are not word-for-word accurate. Emile never said anything about not cleaning Addison's face because she was worried about her own bleeding. She did, however, try to explain why she feared for her own life. To arrive at these quotations, Haddox drew from the handwritten notes Mahle took during his first overnight interrogation of Emile, not her videotaped statements recorded the next day. Nonetheless, by the end of his opening statement, Haddox confidently asserted that the jury would find ample evidence that Emile had purposefully, intentionally suffocated Addison "simply" because she was "not wanted."

Haddox had begun his arguments in a detailed, animated fashion, skillfully minimizing the medical hazards of unassisted childbirth and invoking biased ideals of maternal selflessness. Miller instead opted for brevity and bizarreness. He began by conceding everything: "Did Emile Weaver tell police officers untruths? Did she lie? Yep. She did. She was twenty, nineteen years old, a college student who couldn't go to her mom. She couldn't go to the boy that she thought was the father. She was alone. Did she do the right thing by placing her dead baby in a garbage bag? Absolutely not. Did she do the right thing by trying to hide this? Absolutely not. Did she kill her baby? When you hear the evidence in this case, you will have a reasonable doubt."

After establishing that his client was a liar who couldn't distinguish between right and wrong, Miller turned toward the grotesque: "There's something that's called a hydrostatic test that forensic pathologists perform, particularly on newborn babies, to see whether or not they breathed and their lungs expanded. If their lungs float, then they took at least one breath. We expect him to testify that that breath could have occurred in the womb, in the vagina with the head outside the vagina, or after delivery of the child to tell you that there are other reasonable causes of death other than being placed in a plastic trash bag." Miller conjured this jarring image for the jury without having consulted the state's forensic pathologist, or having any idea how he would testify.

Over the next three days, the prosecution called twenty-five carefully prepared witnesses: eight members of law enforcement, one forensic expert, four members of Muskingum University's administration, and twelve Delta sisters. The prosecution's strategy was

Figure 4.1. Detective Todd Mahle, left, Assistant Muskingum County Prosecutor Ron Welch, and Muskingum County Prosecutor Michael Haddox listen to attorney Aaron Miller's opening statement for Emile Weaver. Weaver is at right.

twofold. First, in order to demonstrate that Emile lacked natural emotions and was untrustworthy, they repeatedly reminded the jury that Emile had failed to act appropriately maternal during her pregnancy and after her labor. Second, they repeatedly described and showed the jury two vivid, memorable images: the first, Addison's corpse inside the trash bag, and the second, her extracted lungs floating in a beaker of water, undergoing the hydrostatic test during the autopsy that Miller had mentioned in his opening statement. In one example of this strategy, Haddox asked Patrolman Mark Stelzer, the first member of law enforcement to arrive on the scene, to identify one of the state's exhibits: "This is a picture of the trash bag I found lying up against the north side of the house," Stelzer replied. "In the bag you can see the right side of the baby's head, mainly the right ear, right side of the face. There's some blood you can see there. And then a little bit of trash that you can see." Haddox took a similar approach during his questioning of Detective K. C. Jones of the sheriff's department, asking him to describe the process of taking the initial crime scene photographs.

> I started with a series of photographs on the outside of the residence but was directed to some trash that was outside on the north side of the residence. And I focused on that for a time.... There was a garbage bag... that was knotted, tied outside.... There was a hole already torn in the side of this bag, and inside you could see the face of a baby. I took photographs of that. And eventually removed the baby from the trash. I laid out a plastic bag on the sidewalk to catch all this, laid the baby on that. It had paper towels, what appeared to be the placenta still with it. It was all kind of stuck together. Laid that out with the baby there on the sidewalk.

The sorority sisters who had discovered Addison's body in the garbage bag were each asked to describe it in exacting detail. The other eight Deltas who testified for the prosecution were asked if they had seen Emile drinking and then given the opportunity to explain why they had been unable to help her during her pregnancy. All twelve sisters made clear that Emile had partied while pregnant, sometimes simply "holding" and other times "sipping" alcohol; that they would have helped and supported her if she had only allowed them to do so; and that now they felt as if they did not truly know her.

One Delta testified that she heard "three or four" infant cries the night of Addison's birth. When asked during Miller's cross-examination why she had failed to mention these sounds in her initial police report, she claimed she was exhausted when she was asked to write the statement and, at the time, thought the sounds were coming from somebody's cell phone upstairs.

Haddox stepped in with a redirect examination, the questioning of a witness that follows a cross-examination:

HADDOX: Were you tired?

DELTA: Yes, I was.

HADDOX: Upset?

DELTA: Sorry. Yes. Very upset.

HADDOX: Are you a police detective?

DELTA: No.

HADDOX: You ever written out a statement like this?

DELTA: No.

HADDOX: You ever investigated a crime?

DELTA: No.

HADDOX: Did you do the best you could do?

DELTA: Yes. At the time I believed it was the best.

Being unemotional, playing dodgeball, and taking black cohosh pills hardly amount to direct evidence of homicidal intent, however, so Haddox also leaned on testimony by Dr. Charles Jeffrey Lee. In his role as the Licking County Coroner, Lee performed and wrote a report on Addison's autopsy—after being told by local law enforcement that Addison had been found in a tied garbage bag, information that likely affected his conclusions about her death. Neither side drew attention to this context. To simplify Lee's technical testimony, which might otherwise be murky or inaccessible to the jury, Haddox lingered over photographs of Addison's hydrostatic "float" test, projected on a large screen for the jurors, which showed a set of miniature lungs buoyant in a clear beaker of water.

"The first question that everyone wants to know," Haddox said, "is was Baby Weaver born alive? "Yes—to a reasonable degree of medical certainty," Lee said. Addison had no obvious injuries and was otherwise "pink and healthy looking," and had therefore died from "asphyxia."

Haddox then asked if Lee had performed any "test of the lungs." "Oh, yes. Yes. We did a very old-fashioned test," Lee responded. "First done probably in the 1800s or 1700s. It's called . . . well, I don't know what it's called . . . the float test." Recalling the technical term "hydrostatic test," Lee elaborated:

> I always heard it called the "float test" because that's easier than "hydrostatic." But yes. Some things float and some things sink in water. So if we take out the lungs and we put them in a cup of water and they float to the bottom, that's what a liver does or that's what a kidney does because there's no air in a liver and a kidney, it will sink. If we put a lung in there and it sinks, then we know there's not enough air to get it to float. If we put it in there and it floats, then we know there's some air in there. We combine that with the X-ray and we see that there's a lot of air in both of these lungs.

Haddox pointed to photographs of Addison's hydrostatic test. "Are those the two lungs?" he asked Lee. "Yes," Lee said, "and that's just a cup of water and they're both floating. And they would float there all day." "Hypothetically, had this child been taken to a fire department less than half [a] mile away and handed over," Haddox asked, "would she have lived?" "Certainly within a reasonable period of time, yes," Lee replied.

Lee's insistence that Addison could have been surrendered safely at a nearby fire station could have been further explored by Miller in his redirect. Instead of addressing the real problems with Lee's logic, however, Miller focused his redirect on the perverse: "Would you agree that a child may cry in the uterus or the vagina, which may

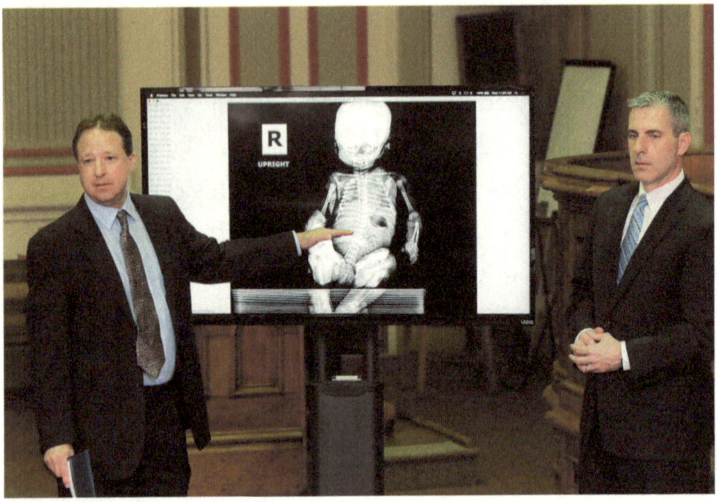

Figure 4.2. Dr. Jeffrey Lee explains an X-ray of baby Addison Grace Weaver. At right is Assistant Muskingum County Prosecutor Ron Welch.

be heard by bystanders in the room or even outside the room?" This question drew an immediate objection. Judge Fleegle allowed Miller to rephrase: "In your education in pathology, are you familiar with the recognition of a child crying or breathing inside the female body?" Lee replied with disbelief: "I've never heard of any child crying, because they're surrounded by water or amniotic fluid. I don't think it would be possible. You can breathe one time in the birth canal, but it's so tight it will compress your chest and you can't expand for a second breath." Undeterred, Miller pressed on.

MILLER: If the membranes rupture and air has entered the uterus, would that enable a child to cry?

LEE: I've never heard of that. I've never experienced that.

MILLER: Would you agree that an autopsy may provide strong but not definite evidence of a live birth?

LEE: Yes, I would agree with that.

MILLER: The fact that lungs float indicates simply that a child took one or more breaths, correct?

LEE: No.

MILLER: That is not correct?

LEE: Not just one or more. It takes several breaths, some say many breaths, to get to the point where there's enough air in there to float. One breath is not going to be enough.

MILLER: All right. Would you agree that the flotation test is not absolute proof of a live birth?

LEE: If that's the only thing you are looking at, I would agree with that test.

MILLER: Would you agree that a child can breathe while its head is in the vagina?

LEE: Like I said, you can take one breath, but then the chest is so compressed there's not enough expansion that she can do to get another breath in.

MILLER: Would you agree that a child can breathe with its head protruding from the vagina?

LEE: Once the chest gets out then I would agree with that, but no more than once inside the birth canal, while the chest is in the birth canal.

MILLER: Would you agree that a child who has breathed in the vagina or with its head outside of the vagina could die from natural causes?

LEE: Certainly.

On Friday morning, the prosecution rested its case. Miller asked that Emile be acquitted on the charge of aggravated murder; even if the court construed the evidence most strongly in the prosecution's favor, he argued, the state had failed to show that Emile had acted purposefully. Haddox countered that he had introduced "plenty" of evidence and that a jury "could reasonably find both purpose and recklessness" in Emile's actions. Fleegle agreed with the prosecution. Emile's motion to acquit was denied within a matter of minutes. Miller called one witness to testify in Emile's defense: Emile.

MILLER: You are in the Muskingum County Jail; is that right?

WEAVER: Yes.

MILLER: Now, Emile, who are your mom and dad?

WEAVER: Sandra Potts and Michael Weaver.

MILLER: And it's my understanding your dad's now deceased; is that right?

WEAVER: Yes.

MILLER: How long has he been deceased?

WEAVER: It'll be ten years in October.

MILLER: How old were you when he died?

WEAVER: Eleven.

MILLER: Now, Emile, did you graduate from high school?

WEAVER: Yes.

MILLER: How did you do in school?

WEAVER: Good. I was on [the] National Honor Society.

MILLER: Were you involved in any sports or those kind of things?

WEAVER: I played basketball and softball.

MILLER: Where did you graduate in your class? Do you know what your rank was?

WEAVER: I was seventh in my class.

MILLER: And you decided to go to college; is that correct?

WEAVER: Yes.

MILLER: Why did you pick Muskingum?

WEAVER: Well, I'm horrible with directions, so Muskingum University is like a small campus. Everything is easily located.

I like that. It was like a small-knit community because that's more what I'm used to back at home. It was an easier driving distance . . . to my house, so if I ever wanted to go home, I could. It was easily obtainable.

MILLER: And what year did you start?

WEAVER: I started August. I do believe it was 2013.

MILLER: August of 2013. Did you have a boyfriend at that time?

WEAVER: I was kind of seeing someone, but it was an off-and-on-again relationship.

MILLER: Who was that?

WEAVER: Brian B.

MILLER: Now, you went through your freshman year—

WEAVER: Yes.

MILLER: During the summer between your freshman and sophomore years, were you still seeing Brian B?

WEAVER: Well, he lives in Cincinnati and I live in Clarington, Ohio, so it was like a four-and-a-half-hour distance. And at the beginning of the summer, we had some problems, so it wasn't like a serious . . . We still talked and hung out and stuff, but I wouldn't consider it an actual relationship.

MILLER: During that summer, did you have sex with Brian B?

WEAVER: Yes.

MILLER: You know Brian A?

WEAVER: What?

MILLER: Do you know Brian A?

WEAVER: Do I know Brian A? Yes.

MILLER: How do you know him?

WEAVER: I met him at Muskingum University.

MILLER: Was he eventually your boyfriend?

WEAVER: Yes.

MILLER: During what period of time?

WEAVER: We met the first day of college, so from that point on. I mean, we didn't start dating for like a month or two later, but . . .

MILLER: Did you have a sexual relationship with him?

WEAVER: Yes.

MILLER: When you started school in the fall, the beginning of your sophomore year, did you know that you were pregnant?

WEAVER: No.

MILLER: Why not?

WEAVER: I just had no idea. I felt the same. I acted the same. There was no indication whatsoever.

MILLER: Did you still have a period?

WEAVER: Yes.

MILLER: As you get toward the winter of your sophomore year, before winter break—

WEAVER: Uh-huh.

MILLER: —did any of that change? Did you have any indication that you were pregnant?

WEAVER: No. I mean, I had an idea, yes. Before winter break?

MILLER: Well, what gave you that idea?

WEAVER: I didn't, like, increase periods . . . like I start . . . spotted through the whole thing, so that had me concerned. But the obvious signs weren't there. So there was a thought process in my mind, but I didn't completely . . . I wasn't completely sure.

MILLER: And when you say the other symptoms and things weren't there, what are you talking about?

WEAVER: I wasn't gaining weight. I still wore the same size clothes. There was no morning sickness. I wasn't tired.

MILLER: At some point after going back to school, did your mind change about whether you were pregnant or not?

WEAVER: I suspected it a little more.

MILLER: Now, at some point in time you went to the wellness center; is that right?

WEAVER: Yes.

MILLER: Tell us about that. How did that come about?

WEAVER: I originally went to the wellness center to get birth control.

MILLER: Why were you getting birth control?

WEAVER: To just . . . you know, if I ever was in a sexual relationship . . . I wasn't at the time and I wasn't planning to be because after the rough relationship I just got out of, but it was just, you know, precautionary.

MILLER: Did you hear people talk about letters that were sent to you and texts and e-mails and things, yesterday and the day before?

WEAVER: Yes.

MILLER: What did you do with that information? Did you ever receive it?

WEAVER: Yes.

MILLER: Did you look at it and read it?

WEAVER: No.

MILLER: Why didn't you read it?

WEAVER: Because I had no indication or felt like at the time that I needed it or needed to know.

MILLER: And why not?

WEAVER: I think I was scared. I felt like I didn't want to know, so I just put it off.

MILLER: Now, you testified that you had a rocky relationship with someone. Who was that rocky relationship with?

WEAVER: Brian A.

MILLER: How would you describe your relationship with him?

WEAVER: It was very controlling and judgmental. My life surrounded around him. The sorority I was in wasn't good enough. He didn't approve. It wasn't the most popular sorority on campus, so it wasn't acceptable for me to be in it. So I really wasn't a part of the sorority as much. I mean, I attended the necessary, like, required events, but other than that it . . . wasn't in it. The new, close friends I did have, his name is Aden and Charlotte, who was here [to testify]. Charlotte's gay and that's not acceptable in his eyes. Aden is black and [Brian A] was very racist, so he was always making judgmental comments towards those friendships I had. And he got drunk and then he was more abusive. He had pushed me around, you know, if I wasn't doing what he said or thought. It just wasn't acceptable. He would push me. He would destroy my room. You know, anything so he had the upper hand.

MILLER: Did you and he ever talk about being pregnant?

WEAVER: Yes.

MILLER: How did those discussions go?

WEAVER: He wanted no part. He acted, you know, like it was all my fault, you know. He didn't want me to tell anyone, because I tried to talk to him about it because I didn't know what else to do, and you know, his reaction was, baseball season was coming and that was his main priority and nothing else.

MILLER: Had you ever discussed getting an abortion with him?

WEAVER: Yes.

MILLER: Did you know at the time you had that discussion that you were actually pregnant?

WEAVER: No.

MILLER: Did you plan to go somewhere to see if you were pregnant?

WEAVER: Yes.

MILLER: Where did you plan to go?

WEAVER: Planned Parenthood in Columbus.

MILLER: Did you actually make that trip?

WEAVER: No.

MILLER: Why not?

WEAVER: There was . . . I don't know if it was an ice storm . . . it was some type of storm, and so, when we finally got onto the main highway, it was shut down.

MILLER: Did you ever follow up with that?

WEAVER: No.

MILLER: Why not?

WEAVER: Because I didn't want to go alone and Brian A told me baseball season was more important and that he had no other time.

MILLER: All right. Let's jump ahead into the spring of 2015. Okay?

WEAVER: Okay.

MILLER: Were you attending parties and those kinds of things as part of your sorority activities?

WEAVER: Yes.

MILLER: Were you consuming alcohol?

WEAVER: I may have took a drink now and then, but that's about it.

MILLER: Were you the kind of girl in the sorority, during the spring, who was consistently getting drunk at parties and those kinds of things?

WEAVER: Yes.

MILLER: Was that early on?

WEAVER: Yes, at the very beginning.

MILLER: Give me some dates. Give me some months.

WEAVER: Probably August when school first started; August, middle . . . beginning of September.

MILLER: Okay. Now, that's fall. I'm talking spring.

WEAVER: Oh, in the spring. No.

MILLER: Okay. Why not?

WEAVER: Because it just . . . I didn't . . . I was . . . I didn't really want to. I just felt like, you know, if there was a possibility . . . you know, I kind of had a feeling I was pregnant, so if it was for sure then I just didn't feel like it was necessary to drink and party.

MILLER: All right. Did you participate in other activities, like during Greek Week?

WEAVER: Yes.

MILLER: Did you participate in dodgeball?

WEAVER: Yes.

MILLER: Did you go to the big party?

WEAVER: Yes.

MILLER: Did you go to the formal?

WEAVER: Yes.

MILLER: Did you get drunk at those things?

WEAVER: No.

MILLER: When you were playing dodgeball, were you trying to terminate your pregnancy?

WEAVER: No.

MILLER: Now, let's go to April 21st of 2015. Okay?

WEAVER: Okay.

MILLER: Once you get into the morning hours of April 22nd, 2015, can you tell us what happened when you woke up that morning.

WEAVER: I woke up, I went downstairs to the kitchen and got a glass of water, and then I proceeded into [the] small bathroom, study bathroom, and I went and sat on the toilet because I felt like I had to poop.

MILLER: What happened after that?

WEAVER: Then after that I felt some pressure lower, and that is when I realized that I was delivering my baby.

MILLER: When you saw that you were delivering the baby, can you describe that for us.

WEAVER: Well, I just pushed once and then the head and everything mostly came out. I think I helped with her shoulder, to help pull her out into the toilet. And then she was in the toilet. Like, her head was upright and everything. And then after that it was . . . I was bleeding really, really bad and that's when I noticed the placenta cord still in.

MILLER: Still in your body?

WEAVER: Yes.

MILLER: What did you do then?

WEAVER: And then I started to panic because I really didn't know what to do, so I started pulling on the cord. And then eventually that's when it came out.

MILLER: So both the baby and the placenta are in the toilet at that time?

WEAVER: Yeah.

MILLER: What did you do then?

WEAVER: Then I got . . . I don't know if it was toilet paper or paper towels, because I was using both throughout the process at that time. So I went and I . . . either one of them I was stuffing up in my vagina area to try to prevent all the bleeding.

MILLER: How would you describe the bleeding to us?

WEAVER: It was more than a normal period. It was, like, heavy. I was . . . it was more than I've ever seen before come out of me.

MILLER: After you stopped trying to fix the bleeding problem, what do you do then?

WEAVER: Uh-huh. Then I went to the kitchen to get a knife.

MILLER: What did you do then?

WEAVER: I went back in the bathroom and I cut the cord between the placenta that was attached to the placenta and the baby.

MILLER: And after you cut the cord, what did you do?

WEAVER: Then I took the baby out and laid her on the floor.

MILLER: When you looked at the baby in the toilet, was the baby moving?

WEAVER: Yes.

MILLER: Where was she moving?

WEAVER: Her ankle was moving.

MILLER: Were her arms moving?

WEAVER: No.

MILLER: Was she kicking or anything like that?

WEAVER: No.

MILLER: Did you notice the baby breathing at that time?

WEAVER: I think her chest was moving very slightly.

MILLER: Was she making any noise?

WEAVER: It wasn't a crying noise. It was more of like a wheezing or gurgling sound.

MILLER: When you picked the baby up, did she move any more than she was moving in the toilet?

WEAVER: No.

MILLER: Did she make any more noise than she did when she was in the toilet?

WEAVER: No.

MILLER: Did her breathing change in any way?

WEAVER: No.

MILLER: And I'm talking about while you're holding her.

WEAVER: Uh-huh.

MILLER: Did you notice any change in the baby at all at that time?

WEAVER: No.

MILLER: All right. Now, after you placed the baby on the floor, what do you do then?

WEAVER: That's when I tried to flush the placenta.

MILLER: Why did you try to flush the placenta?

WEAVER: Because it was terrifying looking. I just wanted it away.

MILLER: What do you do then?

WEAVER: Then I threw the placenta in the trash can. I got some more paper towels and stuffed them back in my vaginal region, and then I sat on the floor with my baby.

MILLER: When you were on the floor with your baby, was the baby left on the floor, or were you holding her?

WEAVER: I picked her up and was holding her.

MILLER: How were you holding her?

WEAVER: Like facing me, like this [*indicating*].

MILLER: When you picked her up, when she was on the floor, did you . . . was she making any noise?

WEAVER: Huh-uh.

MILLER: You—

WEAVER: No.

MILLER: Thank you. It's easier for the court reporter to take down a "no" rather than a "huh-uh." Okay? Were her arms moving or anything?

WEAVER: No.

MILLER: Were her legs moving?

WEAVER: No.

MILLER: Did you notice whether or not she was breathing at that time?

WEAVER: No.

MILLER: Now, you never told that to the detective about holding the baby when she was on the floor.

WEAVER: No.

MILLER: Why not?

WEAVER: I was scared, so I just tried to keep my answers short as possible.

MILLER: What were you afraid of?

WEAVER: I wasn't . . . I was afraid that they were going to find me guilty of this. I mean, I should be found guilty of what I did do, so I did dispose and do everything wrong. So I tried, you know, to explain the things I did wrong.

MILLER: All right. Eventually, did the baby end up in the trash pail with the placenta?

WEAVER: Yes.

MILLER: Was the baby crying or anything at that time?

WEAVER: No.

MILLER: Was she making any noise?

WEAVER: No.

MILLER: Was she moving in any way?

WEAVER: No.

MILLER: Did you tie that trash bag?

WEAVER: I can't say for one hundred percent sure.

MILLER: You just don't remember?

WEAVER: I don't remember.

MILLER: All right. Did you have a car on campus?

WEAVER: Yes.

MILLER: But you do remember just sitting this trash bag right outside the door?

WEAVER: Yes.

MILLER: All right. Eventually EMTs show up. We've heard testimony for two days of you saying that you didn't know that you were pregnant and that you didn't have a baby and that you didn't need help.

WEAVER: Yes.

MILLER: You lied, didn't you?

WEAVER: Yes.

MILLER: Why did you do that?

WEAVER: I was scared. I felt like I had no one and I was worried about, you know, getting in trouble.

MILLER: Why didn't you tell your mom?

WEAVER: With my mom I just kept everything personal that was going on with me, anything bad, I never told my mom because we have different opinions on things. She's more opinionated and overpowering and likes things her way, so I was just too scared.

MILLER: Why didn't you tell your sorority sisters?

WEAVER: You know, because at twenty and being in college with your peers, it's not acceptable. I mean, people can say it's acceptable, but when you're in college it's not. The rumors, you know, are even worse. They talk about you even more. Actually, the girl I talked about in my interview was pregnant, and each and every day I sat at a table with them and they talked about her all the time, either her weight gain or, I mean, I can't believe she's pregnant in college. And I heard it every day, so I just didn't want to tell them. I didn't want to be that person that was even talked about.

MILLER: Now, you have heard people talk about your demeanor.

WEAVER: Yeah.

MILLER: Does that describe you accurately . . . pretty typically depict how you are, as being a calm, laid-back kind of person?

WEAVER: Yeah.

MILLER: Is it hard for you to show emotion?

WEAVER: Yes.

MILLER: Obviously, you've shown emotion here today. What makes this different?

WEAVER: When you sit back and look at every decision you've ever made that's wrong, it's presented in front of you, it's hard not to be after you finally sat down and processed every single thing you've done. At the time I fully didn't understand. I wasn't really . . . I don't have, like . . . it just wasn't processed. Everything wasn't . . . I didn't realize the extent of everything that was happening at the time. I was panicked. You know, I was lightheaded. And so, now that I have the time, you know, to just go back and look at everything, I wish I could have changed and every mistake I made that could have been different. It's a lot harder.

MILLER: What do you wish you could have changed?

WEAVER: I wish I would have, you know, yelled for help. You know, just told someone from the beginning when I had concerns. You know, just everything.

MILLER: Now, there was an officer from Parkersburg who testified yesterday.

WEAVER: Yes.

MILLER: Did you talk to him before, or after you had your D&C?

WEAVER: Immediately after. As soon as I got into my room. He walked in . . . as they're pushing me in my room, he walked in afterwards.

MILLER: Do you remember all the questions that he asked you?

WEAVER: I don't remember any.

MILLER: All right. Emile, I'm going to finish with this. It's the obvious question. I mean, did you put this baby in this green garbage bag in order to suffocate it?

WEAVER: No.

MILLER: Was she already dead, as far as you were concerned, when you put the baby in the bag?

WEAVER: Yes.

With Miller's direct questioning completed, Haddox began his cross-examination:

HADDOX: Ms. Weaver, now let me get this straight. You didn't know you were pregnant but you went to get an abortion, is that what you're telling us?

WEAVER: No. I was going to an abortion clinic.

HADDOX: Why?

WEAVER: To get a further test result and then—

HADDOX: Why?

WEAVER: Why what?

HADDOX: You already had one test result, why are you getting a further one, second opinion?

WEAVER: I didn't look at the first one.

HADDOX: You looked at it, didn't you?

WEAVER: No.

HADDOX: Why did you go get an abortion then?

WEAVER: I didn't go get an abortion.

HADDOX: Why did you go get counseling for an abortion?

WEAVER: I didn't go to counseling to get an abortion. I never made it.

HADDOX: You were on your way?

WEAVER: Yes.

HADDOX: Why?

WEAVER: To get test results.

HADDOX: For what?

WEAVER: To see if I was pregnant.

HADDOX: You already told Brian A you were pregnant.

WEAVER: We discussed it.

HADDOX: You discussed what?

WEAVER: The possibility of me being pregnant.

HADDOX: No, you knew you were pregnant, didn't you?

WEAVER: No.

HADDOX: Don't lie to these people today like you have for nine months. You knew you were pregnant, didn't you?

WEAVER: No.

HADDOX: Say one truthful thing while we're here. You knew you were pregnant, didn't you?

MILLER: Your Honor, it's been asked and answered; object.

FLEEGLE: Sustained.

HADDOX: So why would you go get abortion counseling?

WEAVER: Because if I found out for definite that I was pregnant . . . [it] was probably the path we were going to go.

HADDOX: You just told these people you had no signs of pregnancy. You hadn't gained weight. You didn't feel any different. Nothing was changing about you.

WEAVER: True.

HADDOX: So why were you going to go get abortion counseling?

WEAVER: Because I was going to see if I was pregnant.

HADDOX: You'd already checked. You went to the wellness center September 4th, 2014, didn't you?

WEAVER: Yes.

HADDOX: You looked at your pregnancy test results.

WEAVER: No.

HADDOX: Why?

WEAVER: Because I had no indication that . . . and I didn't feel it necessary to look at.

HADDOX: Why didn't you feel it was necessary to look at?

WEAVER: Because I didn't want to know the answer.

HADDOX: What happened to your birth control pills?

WEAVER: I never got them.

HADDOX: Why?

WEAVER: Because at that point in time there was no . . .

HADDOX: You were pregnant.

MILLER: Your Honor, if he would let her answer the question it might be helpful.

HADDOX: I'm sorry, Your Honor. Go ahead. Why didn't you get your birth control pills?

WEAVER: Because at that point I was in a relationship and after the relationship . . . ours just ended and [I was] not going to get in another one.

HADDOX: You called Brian A down in Cincinnati, didn't you? And you told him you were pregnant?

WEAVER: I told him that it was possible.

HADDOX: And you discussed an abortion?

WEAVER: Yes.

HADDOX: Why would anybody that didn't know they were pregnant talk about an abortion?

WEAVER: I don't know. It wasn't completely confirmed. We were going to get a test and then if the test was confirmed then we were going to probably go on the abortion path after talking.

HADDOX: Do you think that really makes sense?

WEAVER: To me it does.

HADDOX: You never intended to keep this baby, did you?

WEAVER: I didn't have any recollection of what I was going to do with this baby.

HADDOX: Well, did you see a doctor for prenatal care?

WEAVER: No.

HADDOX: Did you share your information with friends?

WEAVER: No.

HADDOX: Did you share this information with family?

WEAVER: No.

HADDOX: Did you have a baby shower?

WEAVER: I don't believe in baby showers.

HADDOX: Did you buy baby clothes?

WEAVER: No.

HADDOX: Did you buy diapers?

WEAVER: No.

HADDOX: Why?

WEAVER: Because I said no so many times that in my mind none of this was happening.

HADDOX: You knew you were pregnant but in your mind you didn't accept it; that's the truth, isn't it?

WEAVER: Yes.

HADDOX: You knew you were pregnant—

WEAVER: I—

HADDOX: —but in your mind you made yourself believe that you weren't, is that what you're saying?

WEAVER: From after winter break, at that point, yes, I made myself—

HADDOX: So—

WEAVER: —not—

HADDOX: So you—

WEAVER: —accept it.

HADDOX: You knew you were pregnant?

WEAVER: No, not when . . . when are you talking about? Can you clarify—

HADDOX: You said after break—

WEAVER: —your question for me, please?

HADDOX: I'm sorry. You said after break I knew I was pregnant, and I'm confirming it. So you're at least admitting at that point you knew you were pregnant; correct?

WEAVER: Yes.

HADDOX: First time we've heard that, isn't it? First time. You never intended to keep this baby, did you? You made no preparation to have a baby, did you?

WEAVER: I made no preparation to have a baby.

HADDOX: Instead, you drank alcohol, correct, while you were pregnant?

WEAVER: I didn't. I took a sip.

HADDOX: A sip?

WEAVER: Yes.

HADDOX: You must have taken a lot of sips because a lot of people saw you holding alcohol at a lot of different parties.

WEAVER: I held alcohol, yes.

HADDOX: Oh, okay. And you smoked marijuana?

WEAVER: One time.

HADDOX: And you took black cohosh?

WEAVER: Yes.

HADDOX: You took eighty of them, didn't you?

WEAVER: I cannot say I took eighty.

HADDOX: You're just not credible, are you?

WEAVER: To the events leading up, no.

HADDOX: No, in general, are you a credible person?

WEAVER: Yes.

HADDOX: Your attorney in opening statement said you're a liar. Even he says you're a liar, didn't he? You lied to people about your pregnancy; correct?

WEAVER: Yes.

HADDOX: You're selective about what you remember and what you don't remember, aren't you?

WEAVER: No.

HADDOX: What were you going to do when this baby came?

WEAVER: I have no idea.

HADDOX: Well, we know that you didn't intend to keep it, correct, because you made no plans to keep it; correct?

WEAVER: Correct.

HADDOX: So option number two would be to hope that you were lucky enough that it was born dead; correct?

WEAVER: That was not—

HADDOX: You took eighty black cohosh pills in—

WEAVER: That was not a thought.

HADDOX: —seventeen days. That was not a thought?

WEAVER: To hope it was dead? No.

HADDOX: So what were your thoughts on what you were going to do?

WEAVER: I didn't think. Like I said before, I had no . . . I didn't think about any of this. I didn't think about the pregnancy. I denied it. In my mind it wasn't happening. There was no further planning for it.

HADDOX: The bottom line is that your baby was born alive, wasn't it?

WEAVER: Yes.

HADDOX: And your baby was breathing?

WEAVER: Yes.

HADDOX: And your baby was moving?

WEAVER: Very slightly. Very little.

HADDOX: And your baby was making noises?

WEAVER: What I would consider [a] gurgling, wheezing noise.

HADDOX: It was crying?

WEAVER: No.

HADDOX: If you had a brand-new puppy, would you put it in a plastic bag and tie it shut?

WEAVER: No.

HADDOX: Why not?

WEAVER: Because it's not—

HADDOX: Why not?

WEAVER: It's not the right thing to do.

HADDOX: Why? What would happen to the puppy?

WEAVER: It would die.

HADDOX: It would die. You researched on the Internet how to terminate a pregnancy, didn't you?

WEAVER: At the very beginning.

HADDOX: You did at the beginning. Why?

WEAVER: Because this is when I was going through thinking of an abortion.

HADDOX: When you had the baby, why didn't you yell for help from your sorority sisters?

WEAVER: I was just panicked and I wasn't thinking correctly.

HADDOX: Why didn't you call 911?

WEAVER: 911 scares me. Clearly, they don't save everyone since they didn't save my father, so I have a weird . . . I don't like doctors. I don't like . . .

HADDOX: Oh, come on, Emile.

WEAVER: Okay.

HADDOX: You just told your counsel if you had to do it all over again, you'd call 911. Why didn't you call 911?

WEAVER: Because I was scared.

HADDOX: Scared of what?

WEAVER: Scared of what people think, scared of what was happening. I wasn't making clear decisions.

HADDOX: So you threw your baby in the bag and suffocated it?

WEAVER: No.

HADDOX: Set it outside, didn't you?

WEAVER: No.

HADDOX: You purposely did not seek prenatal care; correct?

WEAVER: I would not say purposely.

HADDOX: You purposely took black cohosh; correct?

WEAVER: Yes.

HADDOX: You purposely drank alcohol during the pregnancy, couple sips; right?

WEAVER: Yes.

HADDOX: You purposely smoked marijuana during your pregnancy; correct?

WEAVER: Yes.

HADDOX: You purposely concealed the birth of the baby; correct?

WEAVER: Yes.

HADDOX: You purposely did not yell for help during its birth?

WEAVER: I didn't purposely not yell.

HADDOX: Why didn't you?

WEAVER: I didn't yell but it wasn't . . . you know, I wasn't . . .

HADDOX: You intended to yell but you couldn't yell?

WEAVER: No, I just . . .

HADDOX: You didn't yell?

WEAVER: I was just reacting a different way than you would react.

HADDOX: The fact that the baby started to cry, you stopped it, didn't you?

WEAVER: The baby didn't cry.

HADDOX: You purposely did not call 911?

WEAVER: I did not call 911.

HADDOX: And then you purposely place your beautiful baby girl in a plastic trash bag; correct?

WEAVER: Yeah.

HADDOX: And then you purposely tied the trash bag shut tightly with a knot; correct?

WEAVER: I don't remember that part.

HADDOX: You don't remember that part. And then you purposely placed the trash bag with your daughter out with the garbage; correct?

WEAVER: I sat her outside.

HADDOX: On purpose; correct?

WEAVER: Yes.

HADDOX: And even you, you would find yourself guilty, wouldn't you?

WEAVER: Of putting her in the trash bag, yes, how I abused the corpse . . .

JUDGE FLEEGLE: Go ahead. You can play it . . . yes. [*A clip of a recorded phone call from the county jail is played to the jury.*]

HADDOX: Whose voices are those?

WEAVER: I think they're me and my mom.

HADDOX: You know they're you and your mom.

WEAVER: I mean, it was hard to hear, so—

HADDOX: And that's you telling her that you would find yourself guilty?

WEAVER: I would find myself guilty of the crimes that I believe I did, which is the gross abuse of a corpse and the tampering with evidence. Yes, I would find myself guilty to those.

HADDOX: The only problem is, what you put in that plastic bag wasn't a corpse, was it?

WEAVER: Yes, it was.

HADDOX: It was. You checked its vitals? You looked at it carefully? You told us today you didn't even know it was a boy or a girl, all you remember is dark hair. You didn't check its vitals, did you?

WEAVER: No.

HADDOX: You didn't give it CPR, did you?

WEAVER: No.

HADDOX: You knew it was alive, didn't you?

WEAVER: No.

HADDOX: You didn't care, did you?

WEAVER: I did care.

HADDOX: Is that just another one of your lies?

Miller stepped in to redirect:

MILLER: Emile, Mr. Haddox just asked you a question. You didn't answer it. Was that just another one of your lies?

WEAVER: What did he ask me?

MILLER: That you didn't care?

WEAVER: No, I did care.

MILLER: All right. Now, when it comes down to killing this baby, have you lied to this jury?

WEAVER: No.

MILLER: Now, this message between you and Brian A, after the baby was dead, why did you send that? Why did you have that discussion with him?

Figure 4.3. While questioning her on the stand, Muskingum County Prosecutor Mike Haddox shows Emile Weaver a bottle of black cohosh.

WEAVER: I don't know. I was upset. I was angry at everything that happened. And I don't . . . I don't know.

MILLER: Were you angry with him?

WEAVER: Yeah.

MILLER: Did you want to make him feel a certain way as a result of this?

WEAVER: Yeah.

MILLER: How did you want to make him feel?

WEAVER: Just as bad as I felt.

MILLER: Would you agree that you have told all kinds of lies during this case?

WEAVER: Yes.

MILLER: Have you cleared those up here today for these good people?

WEAVER: Yes.

MILLER: Now, you understand that we're not dealing with a puppy; right?

WEAVER: Yeah. It's worse.

MILLER: Why didn't you take vitals?

WEAVER: I don't really know how to take vitals.

MILLER: Why didn't you give CPR?

WEAVER: I don't know how. I feel like I probably would have caused more damage. I don't know how to do CPR, either.

MILLER: When the baby was placed in the big trash bag, was she alive as far as you knew?

WEAVER: No.

The defense rested. The jury recessed. In closing, Haddox spoke first, and at great length. He revisited each witness's testimony in granular detail, emphasizing Emile's alleged unemotional, indifferent nature. Emile knew full well that she was about to go into labor, he argued, and had prepared to kill the newborn by bringing the garbage bag and knife into the bathroom with her. He acknowledged that perhaps it was uncomfortable for the jury to watch him interrogate Emile on the stand. Perhaps some felt sympathy for her. But "sympathy is not a defense," he repeated several times. And Emile's discomfort during the trial was the outcome of her choice to "lie and lie and lie and lie." Her pregnancy denial was laughable; he asked if the mothers on the jury could imagine not knowing they were pregnant. "She wanted Addison dead," Haddox told the jury. "Whether it was during the pregnancy or after her birth, it didn't matter. She didn't want a baby." This was a textbook after-birth abortion.

He instructed the members of the jury to close their eyes and visualize baby Addison alive: "Open your eyes when you can see her." "Murder victims can't speak for themselves," he insisted. "They need a voice, and that voice is justice. We're asking you to give sound to that voice."

For his closing remarks, Miller told the jury: "I'm not going to retry this case. I'm not going to go through what every witness said." Instead he pointed cynically to the prosecution's closing strategy: "If you don't have facts and you have to guess about what happened, when you're the state of Ohio," he said, "you do two things; you ask a jury to close their eyes and imagine what happened to play to your emotion, and the other thing you do is you attack defense counsel." He continued to excoriate the prosecution's tactics: "The state presented witness after witness after witness to testify about everything except this child's death. She drinks. She goes to Greek Week. She plays dodgeball. She does all these things with her sorority sisters. Why? Because if, based on those activities, you hate Emile Weaver, you'll convict her of aggravated murder, that's why. And that is not how our system is supposed to work."

He reiterated his admission that Emile had lied, but noted that she had been consistent in describing the ordeal of the birth and its aftermath. He reminded the jurors that rather than charging her with intentional murder, they could consider the lesser offense of reckless homicide. "Every time I stand in front of a jury I get a sick feeling, queasy," he told them. "I always wonder, have I done everything that I can do to defend my client to the best of my ability? Have I been fair to her? Have I been fair to the court? Have I been fair to you as jurors? Ladies and gentlemen, she's charged with aggravated murder, but that's not what she should be convicted of here. I know it's an emotional case, but I know that you will not take the easy way out."

In his final rebuttal, Haddox again showed the jury the photograph of Addison in the garbage bag: "This photograph represents

Addison's fight, her small mouth open and gasping for the last little bit of oxygen in that dark plastic bag," he told them. "Evidence of a strong will to live, shared by all human beings. But despite her will, she could not overcome her mother's will to kill . . . Why does she not want to remember tying that bag?" he asked of Emile. "Because it was the same as pulling a trigger on a gun, that's why. She put her in that bag and tossed that baby out like trash. There has been no credible testimony or evidence presented to you for you to arrive at any conclusion other than Addison Grace Weaver was purposely killed by her mother."

The jury began deliberating at 3:27 P.M. At 4:45 P.M., they reached a unanimous verdict: guilty on all of the state's charges, including aggravated murder.

On Monday, June 27, 2016, a little over a month after the trial, Emile returned to the courthouse, shackled and wearing the state's orange jumpsuit, for her sentencing hearing. Haddox claimed that Emile had committed "the worst of the worst" offense, given the victim's age and her relationship to Emile. Miller argued that "between two and two hundred" similar "neonaticides" occur each year, amounting to "a social problem" unlikely to be deterred by Emile's sentence, harsh or otherwise. Emile told the judge that she had not yet been able to find forgiveness for herself. Fleegle responded: "It was said more than once that you were more concerned for your own safety than that of the baby's . . . The Court got to see and read the text message you sent later that day that you 'took care of the problem.' That was probably the most truthful statement you made that entire day. You did take care of your problem. It was a problem to you. It was an inconvenience, and you took care of it." He paused to read from a letter Emile had written to him expressing her remorse: "Each day I am spared, I feel remorse. I wake up, I remember. I feel the weight of Addison's absence." Unmoved, Fleegle counted Emile's use of personal pronouns in the letter:

> In those four short paragraphs, you mention "I" fifteen times, and "my" five times. Once again, it's all about you. The Court finds that you committed the worst form of the offense. It's aggravated murder based upon the age of the victim. You can't get any younger than this victim, so it's the worst form of the offense. As indicated by the prosecutor, your relationship to the victim caused it. It was your own child. Mothers are supposed to protect and nurture their children, not kill them just because it was inconvenient. The Court is going to order that you be sentenced to life without the possibility of parole.

The same year Emile was convicted, another Delta sister's pregnancy progressed unrecognized. When labor began, the sister assumed she was having a medical crisis and rushed to the ER, which saved her and her baby's life.

CHAPTER 5

No Safe Haven

ADDRESSING THE MISTREATMENT OF NEONATICIDE

Aggravated murder is the single most serious criminal offense. The severe punishment it demands, justified by the desire for retribution and the hope of deterrence, is meant to be reserved for those who kill purposefully. Most neonaticide cases, however, are prompted by a slow-moving, nine-month crisis in plain view of the victim's community. Many suspected Emile was pregnant, as is typical in neonaticide cases. Yet because neonaticide is so misunderstood, no one was equipped with the tools to intervene effectively. At the time of Addison's death, Emile was terrified, dissociating, and injured. Her failure to call for help immediately after laboring in panicked silence and alone was not an act of premeditated murder so much as a tragic mistake. How then did the state prove its case against her? And, in light of the injustice she experienced, how might law and policy around these cases be improved upon in the future?

The prosecutor's case against Emile would have made perfect sense to the jury impaneled in 1689 for Elizabeth Emerson's trial and in 1787 for Alice Clifton's. Emile's culpability, like that of Emerson and Clifton, was determined by circumstantial considerations, including a "want of linens," or failure to procure supplies such as diapers and blankets for the baby prior to labor; by the perception that she led a lewd, slutty lifestyle; by her failure to act appropriately nurturing during her pregnancy; by her inability to express maternal love and grief immediately postpartum; and by her expressions of concern for her own health and safety after laboring alone. All of these considerations prompted the judge to define Emile as selfish and callous and find her responsible for purposefully killing Addison. In essence, Emile's failure to be loving and altruistic in ways that were legible to the public immediately after enduring severe medical trauma was assumed to demonstrate her aggressive intention to kill Addison.

The decision to charge Emile with aggravated murder was not based on a rigorous examination of her culpability for Addison's death that took the latest research on neonaticide into account. Instead, her sentence was driven by public disgust with her lack of conformity to the gender norms that dictate appropriate maternal behavior—a disgust shaped by the enduring American myths detailed in Part I, and by portrayals of women in popular culture and criminology as incapable of violence. Sexist theories and cultural scripts can rob women and girls of their natural aggression, while also securing them more sympathetic treatment. When women and girls are assigned harsh punishments, it is often in reaction to their perceived defiance of gender norms.[1] Emile's case fits into this wider pattern. Her fate was determined by historical sentiments and stereotypes rather than her actual experience of pregnancy and labor. Enough is known now by researchers in this area to quickly dispense with the nonsense that pregnancy is always accurately perceived in a timely manner, or that women are physically capable of laboring alone and then instantly providing safe care to their newborn infants.

Neither victim nor monster, Emile bears culpability for Addison's death. Even in crisis, Emile should have called out for help and now regrets not doing so. It is crucial, however, to examine the context and circumstances of her labor in order to understand these recurring tragedies. Emile's crime is, in part, an unintended consequence of her flawed perception of her situation. Emile knew that she would face stigma if her condition was publicly recognized because, over the course of her pregnancy, she was paying careful attention to the cruel gossip levied at the other single woman on campus whose baby bump was visible and widely mocked. Emile's socialization into femininity predisposed her to value maintaining the appearance of conformity to contradictory gender norms and ideals. She was determined to navigate an impossible tension between the rowdy lifestyle of her peers in college and the religious dictates upheld by the older generation in her family. The responsibilities of maintaining sexual propriety, securing birth control, scheduling prenatal care, and deciding on abortion or adoption all fell on her shoulders. Carrying this weight, the only voice in her ear was Brian's—*does anyone know?*

Emile's story has significant implications for justice and public policy. A troubling throughline connects the treatment of Emile's case by the legal system to cases throughout American history that occurred before the important work of scholars in forensic psychiatry, maternal mental health, and medicine was available. This throughline reveals that even as science advances, legal practice often remains stuck in the past, preferring to draw on centuries-old junk science and circumstantial considerations over cutting-edge inquiry on the obstacles to pregnancy recognition and the significance of unresolved childhood trauma and intimate partner abuse. Simply taking the medical implications of unattended childbirth into account at all stages of the investigation and prosecution of neonaticide cases would improve the quality of justice offered to women like Emile, who should have received medical care before she was interrogated. The legal system must also retire outdated, sexist stereotypes and maternal myths and instead incorporate medical, psychological, social, and cultural factors into sentencing decisions in neonaticide cases.

The uneven success of Emile's post-conviction appeals illustrates the value of testimony from experts on the latest research during sentencing decisions. After Emile's conviction in 2016, her case was taken on by the Ohio Office of the Public Defender's death penalty team. Her new attorneys hired Dr. Diana Barnes, a leading international expert on maternal mental health and the top advocate for recognizing unperceived pregnancy as a formal diagnosis. After eight years of appeals, which reached the Ohio Supreme Court on two different occasions, Emile was granted a resentencing hearing where Dr. Barnes testified at length.[2] She detailed how research on pregnancy denial has recognized the complexities of unperceived pregnancy and noted the mitigating impact of Emile's unresolved childhood trauma and her dissociative state at the time of Addison's death. Despite a barrage of blatantly sexist attacks on her professionalism by the prosecutor, Dr. Barnes's testimony was well received. The hearing culminated in a reduction of Emile's sentence from the maximum (life without the possibility of parole) to the minimum for aggravated murder (life with the possibility of parole after twenty years). While this is certainly a positive, meaningful outcome for Emile and her loved ones, incorporating this enriched understanding of neonaticide years earlier might have altered Emile's initial indictment and conviction.

American women who commit high-profile neonaticides are often charged with aggravated murder. This prosecutorial norm says less about the realities that drive these cases and much more about local politics that favor tough-on-crime spectacles, especially punishment for so-called after-birth abortions, a popular colloquialism for neonaticide. With more pragmatism and nuance and less political performance, most other countries that share U.S. legal norms acted earlier to address infanticide. Between 1920 and 1950, twenty-four countries, including Britain, Canada, and Australia, revised their criminal legal codes to define maternal infanticide as a distinct offense, different from homicide among adults.[3] These laws were informed by early-twentieth-century psychological and medical insights, as well as public sympathy for struggling, stigmatized single women, which made juries unwilling to convict.[4] In consideration of the effects of childbirth and postpartum mental health conditions, sentencing under these laws often includes treatment or noncustodial supervision and limits confinement to between one and five years. In contrast, the American Psychological Association did not recognize the term "postpartum" until 1994 and does not yet recognize pregnancy denial and unperceived pregnancy as clinical diagnoses.[5] Even in cases where mothers are clearly suffering from postpartum psychosis, the American court system often inflicts harsh punishment instead of providing treatment.

In addition to highlighting the need for legal reform, Emile and Addison's story has implications for the future of public policy. The sentiments and stereotypes that Ohio weaponized against Emile in court are consistent with dysfunctional national policies on issues related to infant homicide, abandonment, and mortality. This flawed foundation has had fatal implications.

For years, U.S. lawmakers focused hearings on infanticide solely on femicide in China and India, finally turning to the United States in the 1990s with the introduction of Safe Haven laws. Bipartisan and popular, these laws were inspired by public outrage over high-profile cases like Emile's in which babies were found dead in dumpsters. Unfortunately, these laws were passed by every state without effective implementation strategies or sufficient funding and were misinformed about the root causes driving most child abuse and neglect-related deaths.[6]

While safe surrender can be a lifesaving option for parents in crisis, it is not the right policy to prevent neonaticide. Women, like Emile, for whom these laws were originally passed to assist, are not likely to be able to call for help during their pregnancies because calling a crisis hotline requires a recognition that one is, in fact, in crisis. Emile, and women in her position, tend not to experience the traditional symptoms of pregnancy and, in the absence of decisive signs, become mired in psychic conflict. On the one hand, they fear, perhaps in some cases irrationally, that their community will not recognize them as good mothers and that they will be rejected by their friends and families. Facing stigma while raising their babies alone is an overwhelming, unbearable prospect. On the other hand, they deeply desire the unconditional love the baby represents. The case studies discussed in chapter 2 on Ms. T and the perfectionist high school student as well as anecdotal evidence from those working on the frontlines suggest that women in Emile's position who make it to a hospital emergency department in time to receive medical assistance during childbirth tend to keep their babies and raise them successfully. These women and their families would regret surrendering their babies with no hope of future contact. Emile's intense grief and remorse after losing Addison demonstrate that she was trapped in this impossible double bind.

As a tool for preventing neonaticide, the logistical assumptions underlying safe surrender are also illogical. As the German Ethics Council explains, women at risk for neonaticide are in a "psychodynamic situation [that] precludes the planning and active problem-solving necessary" to utilize Safe Haven laws.[7] Policies that seek to prevent neonaticide *after* women have concealed pregnancies and *after* they have labored alone are, in and of themselves, dangerous and need to be reoriented towards earlier interventions, such as preventing family violence and preventing incest and rape.

After laboring alone, women who are in a dissociative state, bleeding profusely, shocked, and panicked are unlikely to be able to hygienically sever and clamp their babies' umbilical cords and then travel any distance, even a very short one, to reach safe surrender sites such as hospitals or fire stations. Terrified and panicked, they are also unlikely to perceive their newborns accurately or be able to make intentional choices. Like Emile, many women in this traumatized state assume they have miscarried. Almost no young American women have ever been in the presence of a newborn infant who is still coated in vernix and attached to a placenta. (Indeed, even those who have delivered babies in hospitals often don't see their newborns until after the cord has been cut and the vernix removed.) As Emile's testimony highlights, she found being in the presence of her placenta horrifying. Newborns in this state do not resemble, act, or sound like babies even a few hours older.

Infant homicide experts argue that increasing access to numerous public health services and addressing long-running inequities are also vital for prevention. These include mental health care, addiction disorder treatment, intra-family violence mitigation, adoption and safe surrender options with counseling, accurate sex and parenting education, birth control, abortion, nonpunitive respite childcare, and allowing women to deliver babies in hospitals for free while remaining anonymous. Experts and frontline workers agree that a holistic approach to prevention needs to take the well-being of not only babies, but also mothers, families, and communities into account. Yet Safe Haven laws, the main focus of U.S. lawmakers, simply decriminalize infant abandonment under a set of specific terms that vary unpredictably state to state—a move that implies that women like Emile are merely modern-day Charlotte Temples who need relief from shame as opposed to more meaningful support for parenting. Instead of improving the social safety net that supports all families, these laws, when implemented poorly, undermine the ethical guidelines that define modern adoption by facilitating secretive abandonments.

The chasm between what experts deem necessary for prevention and what American lawmakers have actually done raises difficult questions about the relationship between historical amnesia and contemporary political indifference. The historian Richard Hofstadter explains that the ideology of American exceptionalism creates a context within which documenting the role of violence in shaping American power and industry makes little sense.[8] "What is impressive to one who begins to learn about American violence," Hofstadter writes, "is its extraordinary frequency, its sheer commonplaceness in our history, its persistence into very recent and contemporary times, and its rather abrupt contrast with our pretensions to singular national virtue."[9] Hofstadter underscores that our sense of national pride is contingent on overlooking, or denying, the role certain kinds of violence have played, and continue to play, in shaping the structure of our society. Even more taboo than the kinds of institutional and collective violence that Hofstadter documents, infanticide remains a largely unwritten chapter in our national history. The grim picture that emerges from the available accounts, however, makes clear that infant homicide has played a decisive role in the lives of many women and babies and is indicative of their struggles to survive. In this way, infanticide fits into a broader historical pattern in which violence is both part of our national experience and an expression of our "unacknowledged (underground) value structure."[10]

American structural violence also finds expression in staggering rates of infant mortality, not just as enacted through infanticide. Throughout American history, law and public policy have sought to invent an ethical distinction, then direct anger and empathy accordingly, between blameless and blameworthy infanticidal mothers and between infant homicide and state policies that have infanticidal outcomes. This process politicizes sympathy in ways that direct public outrage toward so-called monster mom figures and away from infanticidal state policies that impact all parents and babies. An example of such a policy, literary critic A. Samuel Kimball explains, is one that directs health and educational resources discriminatorily, thereby jeopardizing certain children's well-being. Like a neglectful parent who forgets to secure a child's seatbelt, policies that allow income inequality, racial inequality, the migration crisis, and climate change to rage unmitigated while restricting and stratifying access to health care subject children and babies to "the effects of repeated risk and jeopardy," taking an infanticidal toll.[11]

This toll is most pronounced, not in infant homicide rates, but in the much larger rate of preventable infant deaths. While the politics of abortion perpetually dominate the news cycle, interrupted on occasion by sensationalized neonaticide cases, the fact that the U.S. infant mortality rate is among the highest in the industrialized world is rarely ever discussed. Yet more American babies die during their first day of life than in all other industrialized nations combined.[12] These babies are not neonaticide victims. Instead they are beloved new members of mostly non-white communities that systematically confront obstacles to accessing healthcare and that endure a host of environmental, economic, and social hazards. "Despite the urgency of the problem, there has been little public discussion of infant loss," writes sociologist Monica Casper.[13] "Who cares?"[14] she asks, pointing out how little action has been taken to address these deaths, many of which are preventable, and that very few of those not directly impacted by infant loss are invested in addressing the persistent inequalities that create it.

Conclusion

A SOCIAL THEORY OF NEONATICIDE RISK

To fundraise for both victims of crime and their local crisis pregnancy center, the Delta sisters host an annual five-kilometer Color Run. In 2023, the sorority succeeded, with help from community partners, in raising enough funds to purchase an infant abandonment device (IAD)—a so-called baby box where infants can be surrendered—for Muskingum County. Pictures of the event shared on social media document a fun-filled day, amateur runners in matching tie-dyed T-shirts loping through chalky pastel-colored clouds. A report on the event by FOX5 Zanesville claimed that a local Boy Scout working toward his Eagle rank had brought the idea to the sorority.[1] Perhaps the journalist was unaware of the fundraiser's original inspiration—Addison's death—or had chosen to highlight a more positive story. In leaving Addison and Emile out of the narrative, however, the report missed an opportunity to raise awareness about unperceived pregnancy and its connection to neonaticide risk.

The same year the Deltas purchased their IAD, two devices in other Ohio communities were removed. Ohio's Safe Haven law requires all IADs to be located at sites with personnel present twenty-four hours a day, seven days a week because, according to the Ohio Department of Health, the boxes' silent alarm systems can fail at critical moments.[2] The device's $20,000 price tag does not reflect the true cost of maintenance and staffing.

Local residents regarded the device removals with mixed emotions. Some worried that decommissioning the boxes left women with even fewer options for dealing with unwanted pregnancies. Others argued that their communities needed to do more to help families in crisis and that the boxes might encourage women to hide pregnancies and avoid prenatal care, creating new unintended risks. The debate appears to be largely hypothetical, however: In the nineteen years since Ohio passed its Safe Haven law, only one of seventy-three surrendered babies has been left in a box. As Professor Jessie Hill, an expert in reproductive law, explains, even as these devices "lift the possibility of criminal punishment" and of "social stigma," anonymous abandonment still exacts a heavy "emotional toll," leading many to make a different choice for themselves and their babies.[3]

In a moment when new IADs are being installed while others are being decommissioned, the need for evidence-based, trauma-informed public health policy is increasingly pressing. Experts on infant abandonment and homicide recommend sweeping improvements to the social safety net that would elevate the status of parents and babies in society, as well as more targeted interventions within the medical, mental health, and criminal justice fields. These policy changes would surely benefit many families and improve both infant safety and quality of life. They are not, however, quick or easy fixes. They demand a willingness to "recognize the importance of community, of caring for others, of socialized medicine, and of plowing significant proportions of gross domestic product back into communities to help those left behind," explains Dr. Neil Websdale, a family violence expert, and to confront the "enormous expenditures on the criminal justice juggernaut and incarceration, and an abject failure to connect individual malevolence and pathology to social, economic, and political arrangements" in the United States.[4] As Websdale argues, individualistic national ideals make enacting effective public health policy in this area unlikely. Given this predicament, improved data collection—consistently gathered and publicly reported by all states on all types of infant abandonment and homicide—would be a valuable first step.

In calling for improved data collection, however, I do not mean to overstate the potential for science to prevent future tragedies. Instead, better data would allow for a more accurate accounting of the scope and scale of the problem. Looking at the precarity of victims' lives and the changeable nature of emotions that can lead to hazardous decision-making, Websdale argues against the "objectivist posturing of modern science" that presumes that expert knowledge can calculate risk and improve victim safety. Perhaps, as Addison and Emile's tragedy underscores, it is "wiser to acknowledge the inherent difficulties in predicting human behavior" and instead consider how these limitations might support a more humane practice of justice.[5]

My investigation into Addison and Emile's tragedy demonstrates the limits of empiricism in addressing neonaticides. Numerous social and emotional obstacles to preventing Addison's death appeared in the months before it took place. The more we come to understand these obstacles, the more intractable neonaticide appears to be, especially in the absence of sweeping social and cultural change. And many of these obstacles are exacerbated by social media, which distances the physical body from the socially performed self and encourages users to edit their social image to cover imperfections.

When pressed to explain during her trial why she hadn't opened the certified letter from the student health center with her positive pregnancy test results, Emile's explanations made little sense. She didn't have "any indication" that she was pregnant and didn't feel that she "needed to know." She was "scared." "I felt like I didn't want to know, so I just put it off." As she told me during an interview, she began repeating a mantra to herself after receiving the letter: *This isn't happening to me. It will go away.* If she had opened the letter, she could have ended her pregnancy legally, arranged an open adoption, or organized her support system in preparation for parenting in college. Yet humans are not adept at the kind of pragmatic foresight that opening a letter with potentially life-changing news requires.

Coming to recognize even a wanted, planned pregnancy is still a complex, multistage process for most women, not an instantaneous or obvious binary. Women may consider their pregnancy risk, perceive and interpret signs and symptoms of pregnancy, seek external confirmation by taking a home pregnancy test followed by an ultrasound in a doctor's office, then seek social approval by sharing their pregnancy news. Each step demands great intention. This process of recognition is highly variable and can be understood as a liminal physical and social state that impacts not only women's bodies but also their personhood and identity.[6] Triggered by external stress and internal conflict, women like Emile demonstrate a general tendency to rely on denial as a coping mechanism, validated by a lack of clear physical symptoms of pregnancy. In these cases, women achieve short-term benefits to their social standing and to their sense of self by perceiving themselves as not pregnant. The underlying mental processes that drive this kind of pregnancy denial are indicative of a much broader human difficulty with prospection, or the ability to imagine ourselves in the future and plan appropriately for changes that are beyond our control. Referred to as the "end of history illusion" by social psychologists, who have observed it in people from eighteen to sixty-eight years old, it describes a view of the present as a "watershed moment" in which we have "become the person we will be for the rest of our lives."[7] Even though we are keenly aware of how much our values, personalities, and preferences have changed in the past, we view ourselves in the present as fixed, as final; we wrongly assume that we will barely change in the future. The end of history illusion can have a negative impact on decision-making, often resulting in regret—the primary emotion experienced by women who realize, often in retrospect, that they have committed neonaticide.[8]

Given humans' difficulty with self-prospection, the kind of pregnancy denial Emile experienced can be seen as a psychic and social conflict between a self that is not pregnant in the present and one that is pregnant in the future and thus burdened with stigma. Few life events change one's identity as significantly or have a bigger impact on one's status as pregnancy and motherhood. For women who are ready to start their families and who are viewed as good mothers by their families and communities, embracing a maternal identity can come with emotional rewards and feel like an accomplishment. I recall my own prepregnancy checklist: graduate degree completed, employment with health benefits, romantic partner also eager to parent, stable housing, maternity leave (and extra income for adorable tiny shoes). Without having achieved these metrics, I did not feel able to claim the status of mother, which says a lot about the prosperous, suburban community I grew up in outside of Boston and its emphasis on higher education and professional success. Yet for many, pregnancy and motherhood are fraught with bias and weighted with social costs and stigma, rather than symbols of success and achievement.[9]

Emile's fear of knowing was a reaction to the high social and emotional stakes of her situation, consistent with sociologist Erving Goffman's work on the fragility of humans' performances of self.

Goffman writes that our social lives are a precarious achievement and that the desire to avoid shame, humiliation, and the other painful emotions incited by rejection is an organizing principle behind human interaction.[10] The burden of stigma, he explains, is real for both the stigmatized and the community that disparages them: "We believe the person with a stigma is not quite human. On this assumption we exercise varieties of discrimination through which we effectively, if often unthinkingly, reduce [her] life chances."[11] Goffman's perspective on the burden of stigma helps explain the temporary relief that pregnancy denial and unperceived pregnancy provide. In the absence of physical, publicly recognizable signs of pregnancy, each day of pregnancy denial is a day the pregnant person is shielded from stigma and can thus avoid reckoning with the realities of how their pregnancy will restrict their access to opportunities and diminish their social standing. Women like Emile lean away from stigma, protecting their past and present identity in ways that put their future self and baby at risk. Feelings of isolation and shame—which can be experienced even in the midst of bustling family and sorority life—make it difficult to recognize the autonomy and individuality of others.[12] In neonaticide cases, the mother rarely recognizes the newborn infant's personhood in time.

This sociological perspective on neonaticide is at odds, however, with the traditional cultural scripts that control how cases like Emile's are represented in the public sphere. The categories of mad, bad, and victim deployed by the American press to report on infanticides are not unique to these kinds of crimes or exclusive to journalism and popular culture. As this book details, these narratives are entangled in scholarly research and legal practice. Reports written by professionals working in the criminal justice system, including psychiatrists, probation officers, and parole agents, have been found to describe violence other than infanticide committed by women in ways that negate agency. Several studies have found that even in official case reports, women's crimes are written about as either pathological or demonic. Pathological explanations neutralize women's responsibility for their actions, negating culpability, while reports that demonize women's motives focus on their failure to conform to gender stereotypic expectations.[13] While familiar, these stories are misleading. When asked directly by researchers, incarcerated women explain their motivations for committing acts of violence in the same terms used by men, including the desire for financial gain, respect, and reparation. "Expressions of male and female offending share many similarities," write criminologists Candace Kruttschnitt and Kristin Carbone-Lopez, and "are often determined by the same sorts of personal and political concerns."[14]

Given that professionals working in the criminal justice system tend to rely on stereotypic cultural scripts, it is perhaps unsurprising that even those in closest proximity to these tragedies also come to identify with these tropes. Since Emile's trial, her mother Sandy has given interviews to me and other journalists that focus on her history of intimate partner and intra-family abuse. To defend her daughter, she has opened up about painful aspects of her past that she would have preferred to hide under better circumstances. But given the lack of sympathy extended to Emile, Sandy has found the courage to describe some of her worst life experiences. And she has taken responsibility for how these traumas negatively impacted her relationship with Emile, leading Emile to feel that she couldn't confide in Sandy about her pregnancy fears. Sandy is reckoning with her past and, in doing so, she is explaining Emile's actions as the end result of victimization. She is also attempting to redirect blame away from Emile and toward her own failed mothering. Despite Sandy's efforts to claim the label for herself, however, Emile still tells me and the journalists who interview her that she sees herself as the "monster" depicted in news reports and social media posts on her case.

Perhaps any coherent narrative is preferable over confusion that one's actions or one's daughter's actions are inexplicable—or worse, rational. "We tell ourselves stories in order to live," Joan Didion famously observed. "We live entirely, especially if we are writers, by the imposition of a narrative line upon disparate images, by the 'ideas' with which we have learned to freeze the shifting phantasmagoria which is our actual experience."[15] For Didion, lucidity is a forced, fleeting achievement. Far from suggesting that stories are somehow magical, she instead explains the relief of coherence that narratives offer in the face of the disparate, conflicting experiences that comprise our lives. Noting that our actual experience is one of ever-changing "phantasmagoria," a word that conjures hallucinations, fantasies, and optical illusions, Didion writes that we use the solidity of ideas as protection against the discomfort of incoherence. Through this lens, pregnancy denial appears to be a dangerous manifestation of the mind's habit of making sense of the otherwise inexplicable—an effort to live by a story that feels familiar but is ultimately doomed.

Or perhaps Sandy and Emile are learning, like the women whose cases appear on the historical record, to embrace stereotypes in order to elicit some measure of sympathy. Recognition of stereotypes and a willingness to conform to them might continue to be one measure of agency, albeit a devastating one for Sandy and Emile to internalize. I wish for both mother and daughter a different story and a different sense of self—one that does not have to be blameless in order to be deserving of redemption. It is telling that after being found not guilty for the murder of her baby Annabel, Brooke Richardson's wish was to return to being "normal."[16]

Acknowledgments

Over the challenging years that were needed to write this book, the support of many institutions and individuals helped me persist. In many ways, this book applies my undergraduate training in Smith College's Sociology Department and my graduate training at The George Washington University's doctoral program in American Studies. At the outset of my inquiry, Emile Weaver's and Sandy Potts's informed consent to being research participants was vital. Research travel to Ohio was funded first by the Program in Writing and Rhetoric at Stanford University and later by Dartmouth College's Arts and Sciences and Writing Program. On the ground assistance from the Dayton Correctional Institution and the Ohio Office of the Public Defender were also vital during my fieldwork.

While conducting the historical and archival research for Part I, I was assisted by two librarians at Dartmouth College, Jennifer J. Natale and Wendel Cox, and by Arlene Shaner, the Historical Collections Librarian at the New York Academy of Medicine. I am deeply grateful to behavioral historian Gregory Hanlon and forensic psychiatrist Phillip J. Resnick for in-depth interviews that helped me better understand their perspectives on neonaticide.

During the writing process, I was buoyed by the exacting feedback of writing group partners Jennifer Cho, Charity Fox, Jeannine Love, Melissa Kagen, and Elizabeth Spragins. Later, Sophie Hagen offered inspired edits. My parents, Wendy and Paul Lewis, read an infinite number of drafts encouragingly. My partner and cheerleader, Wayne Greenwood, helped me make the time necessary to write. My children, Ivy and Mars, provided reprieve from the difficulty of the book's subject matter. And childhood bestie, Nira Salant, was, as always, my homebase.

I have also benefited from camaraderie among other researchers and frontline workers. Lori Bruce, Micah Orliss, Emily Douglas, Liisa Speaker, Rachel Wagner, and Noelle Ozimek helped me better understand the difficulties encountered by those on the frontlines and arrive at stronger policy proposals. My perspective is further enriched by maternal mental health expert Diana Barnes, who models the bravery needed to share expert testimony on neonaticide. Finally, I am most fortunate to have the occasion to thank Michelle Oberman who has been a key mentor, friend, and collaborator. Her work and the tenacious way she conducts it are a potent source of inspiration and grit.

Notes

INTRODUCTION

1. Jason Silverstein, "Former Ohio College Student Killed Hours-Old Newborn, Left Her in Trash Outside Sorority House: Cops," *Daily News,* April 9, 2018, https://www.nydailynews.com/2015/07/25/former-ohio-college-student-killed-hours-old-newborn-left-her-in-trash-outside-sorority-house-cops/.

2. Michael E. Miller, "'No More Baby': Sorority Sister Gets Life Term for Tossing Newborn into the Trash to Die," *Washington Post,* June 28, 2016, https://www.washingtonpost.com/news/morning-mix/wp/2016/06/28/no-more-baby-sorority-sister-gets-life-term-for-tossing-newborn-into-trash-to-die/.

3. Danielle Cinone, "Killer's Regret: Sorority Girl Jailed for Life after 'Throwing her Newborn Baby in the TRASH' Now Feels Like a 'Monster,'" *U.S. Sun*, January 16, 2020, https://www.the-sun.com/news/267575/sorority-girl-jailed-newborn-baby-trash-monster/.

4. *Global Study on Homicide, Killing of Children and Young Adults* (Vienna: United Nations Office on Drugs and Crime, 2019).

5. Isabelle Horon and Anne K. Driscoll, "Homicide among Infants in the United States, 2017–2020," *National Vital Statistics Reports* 72, no. 9 (July 2023): 1–10.

6. Barber T. Fujiwara, J. C. Schaechter, and D. Hemenway, "Characteristics of Infant Homicides: Findings from a U.S. Multisite Reporting System," *Pediatrics* 124, no. 2 (2009): e210–e217.

7. Fujiwara et al., "Characteristics of Infant Homicides."

8. Katie Watson and Cara Angelotta, "The Frequency of Pregnancy Recognition across the Gestational Spectrum and its Consequences in the United States," *Perspectives on Sexual and Reproductive Health* 54, no. 2 (2022): 32–37.

9. WLWT5 Digital Staff, "Skylar Richardson Released from Probation, Judge Rules," WLWT5, November 17, 2020.

10. Barbara Barnett, *Motherhood in the Media: Infanticide, Journalism, and the Digital Age* (New York: Routledge, 2016); Ania Wilczynski, "Images of Women Who Kill Their Infants: The Mad and the Bad," *Women Crime and Justice* 71, no. 2 (1991): 73.

11. Aberration, *Oxford English Dictionary* online (Oxford: Oxford University Press, 2024), https://www.oed.com/dictionary/aberration_n?tab=meaning_and_use#11747613.

12. Vestige, *Oxford English Dictionary* online (Oxford: Oxford University Press, 2023), https://www.oed.com/dictionary/vestige_n?tab=meaning_and_use#15801186.

13. Gregory Hanlon, *Death Control in the West 1500–1800: Sex Ratios at Baptism in Italy, France and England* (London: Routledge, 2022).

14. Erkki Koskenniemi, *The Exposure of Infants among Jews and Christians in Antiquity* (Sheffield, UK: Sheffield Phoenix Press, 2009), xi.

15. Laura Hynes, "Routine Infanticide by Married Couples? An Assessment of Baptismal Records from Seventeenth Century Parma," *Journal of Early Modern History* 15 (2011): 507–530.

16. Richard Trexler, "Infanticide in Florence: New Sources and First Results," *History of Childhood Quarterly* 1 (1973): 89–116.

17. Hynes, "Routine Infanticide by Married Couples," 510.

18. Sarah B. Hrdy, *Mother Nature: Maternal Instincts and How They Shape the Human Species* (New York: Random House, 1999).

19. Koskenniemi, *The Exposure of Infants among Jews and Christians in Antiquity.*

20. Hanlon, *Death Control in the West 1500–1800*, 279.

21. Gregory Hanlon, "Routine Infanticide in the West 1500–1800." *History Compass* 14, no. 11 (2016): 543.

22. Hanlon, *Death Control in the West 1500–1800*, 279.

23. Jeffrey S. Adler, *First in Violence, Deepest in Dirt: Homicide in Chicago 1875–1920* (Cambridge, MA: Harvard University Press, 2006).

24. Linda K. Kerber, *Women of the Republic: Intellect and Ideology in Revolutionary America* (Chapel Hill: University of North Carolina Press, 1997).

25. Personal interview with Heather Burner and Michelle Oberman, December 14, 2022, Zoom.

26. Barbara Vobejda, "Study Finds 22,000 'Boarder Babies' in U.S.," *Washington Post*, November 10, 1993.

27. U.S. Department of Health and Human Services, Administration for Children and Families, Administration on Children, Youth and Families, Children's Bureau, "1998 National Estimates of the Number of Boarder Babies," Abandoned Infants and Discarded Infants, https://www.ojp.gov/pdffiles1/Photocopy/191716NCJRS.pdf.

28. James Mohr, *Doctors and the Law: Medical Jurisprudence in Nineteenth-Century America* (New York: Oxford University Press, 1993).

29. Neil Websdale, *Familicidal Hearts: The Emotional Style of 211 Killers* (New York: Oxford University Press, 2013).

30. Websdale, *Familicidal Hearts.*

31. Martin Daly and Margo Wilson's research on contemporary evolutionary theory and the social motives driving homicide is foundational in this area. See Martin Daly and Margo Wilson, *Homicide* (New York: Routledge, 1988) and *The Truth about Cinderella: A Darwinian View of Parental Love* (New Haven, CT: Yale University Press, 1999).

CHAPTER 1 — "INNOCENT AND SEDUCED" VERSUS "LEWD AND CUNNING"

1. John B. Beck, "An Examination of the Medico-Legal Question, Whether, in Cases of Infanticide, the Floating of the Lungs in Water Can Be Depended on as a Certain Test of the Child's Having Been Born Alive," *New York Medical and Physical Journal* 1, no. 6 (1822): 442.

2. John B. Beck, "Address to the Graduates of the College of Physicians and Surgeons of New-York, at the Commencement, Held March 12, 1846" (New York: Henry G. Langley, 1849).

3. Beck, "Address to the Graduates of the College of Physicians and Surgeons of New-York."

4. Michael Sappol, *A Traffic of Dead Bodies: Anatomy and Embodied Social Identity in Nineteenth-Century America* (Princeton, NJ: Princeton University Press, 2002).

5. Beck, "An Examination of the Medico-Legal Question," 444.

6. Beck, "An Examination of the Medico-Legal Question," 444.

7. Beck, "An Examination of the Medico-Legal Question," 445.

8. Marcela Micucci, "'These Demons Who Thirst for Infanticides': Unwanted Pregnancy, Infant Abandonment, and Infanticide in Mid-Nineteenth Century New York City" (PhD diss., State University of New York at Oneonta, 2006); James Mohr, *Abortion in America: The Origins and Evolution of National Policy* (New York: Oxford University Press, 1978).

9. C. R. Gilman, *Sketch of the Life and Character of John Brodhead Beck, M.D., Late Professor of Materia Medica and Medical Jurisprudence in the College of Physicians and Surgeons* (New York: John F. Trow, Printer, 1851).

10. John B. Beck, *Inaugural Dissertation on Infanticide* (New York: J. Seymour, 1817), 47.

11. Beck, "An Examination of the Medico-Legal Question," 441.

12. Beck, *Inaugural Dissertation on Infanticide*, 41.

13. Dustin Griffin, "Cotton Mather and the Emerson Family," *Massachusetts Historical Review* 16 (2014): 9.

14. Gilman, *Sketch of the Life and Character of John Brodhead Beck.*

15. Theodric Romeyn Beck, "Art. I. Annual Address Delivered before the Medical Society of the State of New York," *New York Medical and Physical Journal* (February 6, 1828).

16. James C. Mohr, *Doctors and the Law: Medical Jurisprudence in Nineteenth-Century America* (Baltimore: Johns Hopkins University Press, 1993).

17. Beck, "Art.I. Annual Address."

18. Beck, *Inaugural Dissertation on Infanticide*, 43.

19. Beck, *Inaugural Dissertation on Infanticide*, 43.

20. Katie M. Hemphill, "'Driven to the Commission of This Crime': Women and Infanticide in Baltimore, 1835–1860," *Journal of the Early Republic* 32 (Fall 2012): 442.

21. Thomas A. Crist, "Babies in the Privy: Prostitution, Infanticide, and Abortion in New York City's Five Points District," *Historical Archeology* 39, no. 1 (2005): 19–46.

22. Paul A. Gilje, "Archives: Infant Abandonment in Early Nineteenth-Century New York City: Three Cases," *Signs: Journal of Women in Culture and Society* 8, no. 3 (March 1983): 581; G. S. Rowe, "Infanticide, Its Judicial Resolution, and Criminal Code Revisions in Early Pennsylvania," *American Philosophical Society* 135, no. 2 (1991): 201.

23. Lawrence B. Goodheart, "Changing Legal Culture in the Early Republic: Connecticut, Neonaticide and the Case of Clarissa Ockry," *Connecticut History Review* 53, no. 1 (Spring 2014): 3–15.

24. Amanda L. Miracle, "Intimate Connections: Violence, Patriarchy, and the Law in Seventeenth-Century Maryland Infanticide Cases," *Maryland Historical Magazine* 105, no. 1 (Spring 2010): 6–16; Hemphill, "'Driven to the Commission of This Crime.'"

25. Hemphill, "'Driven to the Commission of This Crime'," 450.

26. Hemphill, "'Driven to the Commission of This Crime'," 453.

27. Goodheart, "Changing Legal Culture in the Early Republic," 3–15; Griffin, "Cotton Mather and the Emerson Family," 1 49.

28. Griffin, "Cotton Mather and the Emerson Family," 9.

29. *Records and Files of the Quarterly Courts of Essex County, Massachusetts* (Salem, 1917), 6:141, in Griffin, "Cotton Mather and the Emerson Family," 8.

30. *Records and Files of the Quarterly Courts of Essex County*, 6:141, in Griffin, "Cotton Mather and the Emerson Family," 8.

31. Griffin, "Cotton Mather and the Emerson Family," 4.

32. Griffin, "Cotton Mather and the Emerson Family," 5.

33. Griffin, "Cotton Mather and the Emerson Family," 6.

34. Griffin, "Cotton Mather and the Emerson Family," 7.

35. Griffin, "Cotton Mather and the Emerson Family," 10.

36. Griffin, "Cotton Mather and the Emerson Family," 10.

37. Suffolk County, file no. 2636, in Griffin, "Cotton Mather and the Emerson Family," 9.

38. Griffin, "Cotton Mather and the Emerson Family," 11.

39. *The Diary of Cotton Mather*, printed in two volumes in the *Collections of the Massachusetts Historical Society*, 7th ser., vols. 7–8 (Boston, 1911–1912), part 1:165; in Griffin, "Cotton Mather and the Emerson Family," 14.

40. *The Diary of Cotton Mather*, part 1:165, in Griffin, 14.

41. Griffin, "Cotton Mather and the Emerson Family," 1.

42. Griffin, "Cotton Mather and the Emerson Family," 1.

43. Rowe, "Infanticide, Its Judicial Resolution, and Criminal Code Revisions in Early Pennsylvania," 227.

44. Rowe, "Infanticide, Its Judicial Resolution, and Criminal Code Revisions in Early Pennsylvania."

45. Rowe, "Infanticide, Its Judicial Resolution, and Criminal Code Revisions in Early Pennsylvania," 227.

46. Rowe, "Infanticide, Its Judicial Resolution, and Criminal Code Revisions in Early Pennsylvania," 229

47. Hemphill, "'Driven to the Commission of This Crime,'" 444.

48. Goodheart, "Changing Legal Culture in the Early Republic," 3–15.

49. Rowe, "Infanticide, Its Judicial Resolution, and Criminal Code Revisions in Early Pennsylvania," 214–226.

50. Hemphill, "'Driven to the Commission of This Crime,'" 444.

51. Miracle, "Intimate Connections," 12.

52. Miracle, "Intimate Connections," 12.

53. Hemphill, "'Driven to the Commission of This Crime,'" 438.

54. Julius Yanuck, "The Garner Fugitive Slave Case," *Mississippi Valley Historical Review* 40, no. 1 (1953): 47.

55. Steven Weisenberg, *Modern Madea: A Family Story of Slavery and Child Murder from the Old South* (New York: Hill and Wang, 1998); Yanuck, "The Garner Fugitive Slave Case," 47–66.

56. Weisenberg, *Modern Madea.*

57. Lucy Stone, "Trial of Margaret Garner," *The Liberator*, February 13, 1856, 1.

58. Lucy Stone, "Trial of Margaret Garner," *The Liberator*, February 13, 1856, 1.

59. Michelle Oberman, "Understanding Infanticide in Context: Mothers Who Kill, 1870–1930 and Today," *Journal of Law and Criminology* 92, no. 3–4 (2003): 707–737.

60. Cliona Rattigan, *"What Else Could I Do?": Single Mothers and Infanticide, Ireland 1900–1950* (Ireland: Irish Academic Press, 2012).

61. Rattigan, *"What Else Could I Do?"*

CHAPTER 2 — THE DISCOVERY OF HETEROGENEITY

1. While the neologism "neonaticide" is Resnick's invention, the observation that women who kill newborn infants immediately at birth are not typically afflicted by mental illness and thus not suited for institutional treatment was discussed in the *Lancet* in 1938. At that time, an astute reader, Hilda Lewis, published a letter to the editor noting that only three out of sixty-four women admitted to the Holloway Sanatorium for killing newborn infants that year had shown "definite signs of insanity" and that two out of the three's conditions had cleared before their trials had begun. See Hilda Lewis, "Infanticide," *The Lancet* (British Edition) 231, no. 5970 (1938): 293.

2. Michelle Oberman, "Understanding Infanticide in Context: Mothers Who Kill, 1870–1930 and Today," *Journal of Law and Criminology* 92, no. 3–4 (2003): 708.

3. Oberman, "Understanding Infanticide in Context," 737.

4. Oberman, "Understanding Infanticide in Context," 737.

5. Cheryl Meyer and Michelle Oberman, *Mothers Who Kill Their Children: Understanding the Acts of Moms from Susan Smith to the "Prom Mom"* (New York: New York University Press, 2001).

6. Kathy Peiss, *Cheap Amusements: Working Women and Leisure in Turn-of-the Century New York* (Philadelphia: Temple University Press, 2001).

7. Lester Adelson, "Some Medicolegal Observations on Infanticide," *Journal of Forensic Science* 4, no. 1. (1959): 63.

8. Kenneth Wheeler, "Infanticide in Nineteenth-Century Ohio," *Journal of Social History* (Winter 1997): 407–418.

9. Elna C. Green, "Infanticide and Infant Abandonment in the New South: Richmond, Virginia, 1865–1915," *Journal of Family History* 24, no. 2 (1999): 205.

10. Karen Brennan and Emma Milne, eds., *100 Years of the Infanticide Act: Legacy Impact and Future Directions* (New York: Bloomsbury, 2023); Josephine McDonagh, *Child Murder and British Culture, 1720–1900* (Cambridge: Cambridge University Press, 2003); Anne-Marie Kilday, *A History of Infanticide in Britain, c. 1600 to the Present* (New York: Palgrave Macmillan, 2013); Nicola Goc, *Women, Infanticide and the Press 1822–1922: Narratives in England and Australia* (Burlington, VT: Ashgate, 2013).

11. Green, "Infanticide and Infant Abandonment in the New South," 205.

12. Simone Caron, "'Killer by Its Mother': Infanticide in Providence County, Rhode Island, 1870–1938," *Journal of Social History* (Fall 2010): 218.

13. Caron, "'Killer by Its Mother,'" 213–237.

14. Karen Majewski, "Abortion and Infanticide in Polish American Detroit and Hamtramck, 1900–1960: A Preliminary Look." *Polish American Studies* 78, no. 1 (2021): 21–40.

15. Majewski, "Abortion and Infanticide in Polish American Detroit and Hamtramck," 26.

16. Majewski, "Abortion and Infanticide in Polish American Detroit and Hamtramck," 38

17. Meyer and Oberman, *Mothers Who Kill Their Children*, 20–27; Diana Barnes, "Towards a New Understanding of Pregnancy Denial: The

Misunderstood Dissociative Disorder," *Archive of Women's Mental Health* 25, no. 51 (2022): 54.

18. Barnes, "Towards a New Understanding of Pregnancy Denial," 54.

19. Interview with Dr. Phillip J. Resnick, Zoom, September 4, 2023, 1–2:30 P.M.

20. Phillip J. Resnick, "Murder of the Newborn: A Psychiatric Review of Neonaticide," *American Journal of Psychiatry* 126 (1970): 46.

21. Resnick, "Murder of the Newborn," 63.

22. Resnick, "Murder of the Newborn," 46.

23. Diane Bernard and Maria Bogen-Oskwarek, "The Maternity Homes Where Mind Control Was Used on Teen Moms to Give Up Their Babies," *Washington Post,* November 19, 2018.

24. Resnick, "Murder of the Newborn," 61.

25. Resnick, "Murder of the Newborn," 61.

26. Resnick, "Murder of the Newborn," 60.

27. Interview with Dr. Phillip J. Resnick, September 4, 2023.

28. Jennieffer A. Barr and Cheryl T Beck, "Infanticide Secrets: Qualitative Study on Postpartum Depression," *Canadian Family Physician* 54, no.12 (2008): 1716–1717.e5.

29. Barnes, "Towards a New Understanding of Pregnancy Denial."

30. Cheryl L. Meyer and Michelle Oberman, *When Mothers Kill: Interviews from Prison* (New York: New York University Press, 2008), 140.

31. Meyer and Oberman, *When Mothers Kill*, 5.

32. Meyer and Oberman, *When Mothers Kill*, 6.

33. Meyer and Oberman, *When Mothers Kill*, 8.

34. N. R. Peacock, M. A. Kelley, C. Carpenter, et al., "Pregnancy Discovery and Acceptance among Low-Income Primiparous Women: A Multicultural Exploration," *Journal of Maternal and Child Health* 5, no. 3 (2001): 109–118; Suzanne O. Bell and Mary E. Fissell, "A Little Bit Pregnant? Productive Ambiguity and Fertility Research," *Development and Population Review* 47, no. 2 (2021): 505–526.

35. Bell and Fissell, "A Little Bit Pregnant?," 505–526.

36. Jens Wessel and Ulrich Buscher, "Denial of Pregnancy: Population Based Study," *British Medical Journal* 324, no. 7335 (2002): 458; Angela Jenkins, Simon Millar, and James Robins, "Denial of Pregnancy: A Literature Review and Discussion of Ethical and Legal Issues," *Journal of the Royal Society of Medicine* 104, no. 7 (2011): 287; Katie Watson and Cara Angelotta,

"The Frequency of Pregnancy Recognition across the Gestational Spectrum and Its Consequences in the United States," *Perspectives on Sexual and Reproductive Health* 54 (2022): 34.

37. Natalia Chechko, Elena Losse, and Susanne Nehls, "Pregnancy Denial: Toward a New Understanding of the Underlying Mechanisms," *Current Psychiatry Reports* 25, no. 10 (2023): 493–500.

38. Doris Vallone and Lori Hoffman, "Preventing the Tragedy of Neonaticide," *Holistic Nursing Practice* 17, no. 5 (2003): 223–228.

39. Paige Neifert, "Denial of Pregnancy: A Case Study and Literature Review," *Military Medicine* 165, no 7 (July 2000): 566–568.

40. Neifert, "Denial of Pregnancy," 567.

41. Neifert, "Denial of Pregnancy," 567.

42. Jeffrey Adler, *First in Violence, Deepest in Dirt: Homicide in Chicago 1875–1920* (Cambridge, MA: Harvard University Press, 2006).

PART II — A DOUBLE TRAGEDY

1. Clara Lewis, "Maternal Violence in an Age of Precarity," Society for the Study of Social Problems national conference, Session 27: Sexuality, Gender and Law, Montreal, Canada, August 2017, https://www.sssp1.org/file/2017/2017AM/Final_Program.pdf.

2. *State v. Weaver*, 2021 Ohio 1025 (Ohio Ct. App. 2021).

CHAPTER 3 — LOSING ADDISON

1. Interview with Emile Weaver, Dayton Correctional Institution, September 20–22, 2017, 12:30–3:30 P.M.

2. These quotations are drawn verbatim from text messages exchanged between Emile and Brian A that are archived in Emile's police file. Emile Weaver's Police File, Ohio Office of the Public Defender, 2015.

3. Natalia Chechko, Elena Losse, and Susanne Nehls, "Pregnancy Denial: Toward a New Understanding of the Underlying Mechanisms," *Current Psychiatry Reports* 25, no. 10 (2023): 499.

4. This inner monologue was relayed to me verbatim during our interview. Interview with Emile Weaver, September 20–22, 2017.

5. I am using the term "it" here to refer to Addison because this is how Emile perceived her in this specific moment in time. Emile's perception changed later and, when it did, she began to refer to Addison by name and as her baby daughter. In my narrative, I change the pronouns to reflect

Emile's changing perception. Among women and girls who experience unperceived pregnancy that leads to neonaticides, Emile is not unique in perceiving her baby as an inanimate "it" in the immediate aftermath of her unassisted labor. This is the most commonly used pronoun in personal accounts across the research literature.

6. *State v. Weaver*, 2021 Ohio 1025 (Ohio Ct. App. 2021).

7. Interview with Emile Weaver, September 20–22, 2017.

8. Emile Weaver's Police File, Ohio Office of the Public Defender, 2015.

9. *State v. Weaver*, 2021 Ohio 1025 (Ohio Ct. App. 2021).

10. This description is based on pictures of the Delta House included in Emile's police file. Emile Weaver's Police File, Ohio Office of the Public Defender, 2015.

11. Mahl's notes, quoted from here, are archived in Emile's police file. Emile Weaver's Police File, Ohio Office of the Public Defender, 2015.

12. Interview with Sandy Potts, Starbuck's Coffee, Dayton, Ohio, September 20, 2017, 5:00–7:00 P.M.

13. Interview with Sandy Potts, September 20.

14. Emile's medical records from her surgery are archived in her police file. Emile Weaver's Police File, Ohio Office of the Public Defender, 2015.

15. Emile Weaver's Police File, Ohio Office of the Public Defender, 2015.

16. C. Jeff Lee's report is archived in Emile's police file. Emile Weaver's Police File, Ohio Office of the Public Defender, 2015.

CHAPTER 4 — LOSING EMILE

1. When I visited the courthouse for a second time in 2023, the bathroom signage had been changed to "Women."

2. Patrick O'Neill and Jessie Balmert, "State Proposes Updates to 11-Year-Old Jail Standards," *Coloradoan*, March 8, 2014.

3. O'Neill and Balmert, "State Proposes Updates to 11-Year-Old Jail Standards."

4. Alex Ronan, "What Did Emile Weaver Know?," *Elle*, January 16, 2020, https://www.elle.com/life-love/a29998766/neonaticide-emile-weaver-sorority/.

5. Jennifer Smola, "Young Women in Muskingum County Who Killed Newborns Got Very Different Sentences," *Columbus Dispatch*, July 9, 2016.

6. Christine Holmes, "Mike Haddox Retires after 35 Years of Fighting for Justice," *Zanesville Times Recorder*, January 3, 2021.

7. Kate Snyder, "5 Years Later: Celest Fronsman Murder Case Stays with Officials," *Zanesville Times Recorder*, September 15, 2017.

8. All direct quotations in this chapter as well as the dialogue that is formatted as script is quoted directly from the transcript of Emile's trial. See *State v. Weaver*, 2021 Ohio 1025 (Ohio Ct. App. 2021).

CHAPTER 5 — NO SAFE HAVEN

1. Candace Kruttschnitt and Kristin Carbone-Lopez, "Moving Beyond Stereotypes: Women's Subjective Accounts of Their Violent Crime," *Criminology* 44, no. 2 (2006).

2. I also read a statement on Emile's behalf during her re-sentencing hearing.

3. Karen Brennan and Emma Milne, eds., *100 Years of the Infanticide Act: Legacy Impact and Future Directions* (New York: Bloomsbury, 2023).

4. Kirsten J. Kramar and William D. Watson, "Canadian Infanticide Legislation, 1948 and 1955: Reflections on the Medicalization/Autopoiesis Debate," *Canadian Journal of Sociology* 33, no. 2 (2008): 237–263.

5. Diana Barnes, "Towards a New Understanding of Pregnancy Denial: The Misunderstood Dissociative Disorder," *Archive of Women's Mental Health* 25, no. 51 (2022): 51–59.

6. Clara Lewis and Michelle Oberman, "Wildly Inconsistent Safe Haven Laws Put Surrendered Infants, Parents at Risk," *Chicago Tribune*, January 11, 2023.

7. Edzard Schmidt-Jortzig, "Anonymous Relinquishment of Infants: Tackling the Problem," Deutscher Ethikrat, 2009, 22, https://www.ethikrat.org/fileadmin/Publikationen/Stellungnahmen/englisch/DER_Stn_AnonKind_Engl_online_Aufl2.pdf.

8. Ira M. Leonard and Christopher C. Leonard, "The Historiography of American Violence," *Homicide Studies* 7, no. 2 (2003): 105.

9. Richard Hofstadter, "Reflections on Violence in America," in *American Violence: A Documentary*, Richard Hofstadter and M. Wallace, eds. (New York: Oxford University Press, 1970), 3–43.

10. Leonard and Leonard, "The Historiography of American Violence," 105.

11. A. Samuel Kimball, *The Infanticidal Logic of Evolution and Culture* (Newark: University of Delaware Press, 2007), 19.

12. Monica Casper, *Babylost: Racism, Survival, and the Quiet Politics of Infant Mortality, from A to Z* (Rutgers, NJ: Rutgers University Press, 2022), 4.

13. Casper, *Babylost*, book jacket.

14. Casper, *Babylost*, book jacket.

CONCLUSION

1. Matt Morris, "Safe Haven Awareness 5K and Color Run," WHIZ Fox5 Zanesville, March 27, 2023.

2. Kendall Crawford, "As Baby Boxes Close, Ohioans with Unwanted Pregnancies Lose Another Option," *Statehouse News Bureau*, April 12, 2023.

3. Crawford, "As Baby Boxes Close."

4. Neil Websdale, *Familicidal Hearts: The Emotional Style of 211 Killers* (New York: Oxford University Press, 2013), 281.

5. Websdale, *Familicidal Hearts*, 275.

6. Katie Watson and Cara Angelotta, "The Frequency of Pregnancy Recognition across the Gestational Spectrum and Its Consequences in the United States," *Perspectives on Sexual and Reproductive Health* 54, no. 2 (2022): 32–37.

7. Jordi Quoidback, Daniel T. Gilber, and Timothy D. Wilson, "The End of History Illusion," *Science* 339, no. 6115 (January 2013): 96.

8. Giulia Milia and Maria Noonan, "Experiences and Perspectives of Women Who Have Committed Neonaticide, Infanticide and Filicide: A Systematic Review and Qualitative Evidence Synthesis," *Journal of Psychiatric and Mental Health Nursing* 29 (2022): 813–828.

9. Jeanine L. M. Skorinko, Angela C. Incollingo Rodriguez, and James K. Doyle, "Overlapping Stigmas of Pregnancy, Motherhood, and Weight: Policy Implications for Employment and Higher Education," *Policy Insights from the Behavioral and Brain Sciences* 7, no. 2 (2020): 123–131.

10. Erving Goffman, *The Presentation of Self in Everyday Life* (New York: DoubleDay, 1959).

11. Erving Goffman, *Stigma: Notes on Impression Management of Spoiled Identity* (New Jersey: Prentice-Hall, 1963).

12. Websdale, *Familicidal Hearts*, 224.

13. Hilary Allen, "Rendering Them Harmless: The Professional Portrayal of Women Charged with Serious Violent Crimes," in *Criminology at the Crossroads*, Kathleen Daly and Lisa Maher, eds. (New York: Oxford University Press, 1998); Edna Erez, "Dangerous Men, Evil Women: Gender and Parole Decision Making," *Justice Quarterly* 9 (1992): 105–126.

14. Candace Kruttschnitt and Kristin Carbone-Lopez, "Moving Beyond Stereotypes: Women's Subjective Accounts of Their Violent Crime," *Criminology* 44, no. 2 (2006): 345.

15. Joan Didion, *We Tell Ourselves Stories in Order to Live: Collected Nonfiction* (New York: Everyman's Library, 2006).

16. Kevin Grasha and Keith BieryGolick, "'I Suffer a Lot': Skylar Richardson's Probation Terminated Nearly 2 Years Early," *Cincinnati Enquirer*, November 17, 2020, https://www.cincinnati.com/story/news/2020/11/17/brooke-skylar-richardson-probation-hearing/6322918002/.

Index

The letter f *following a page number denotes a figure.*

About the Author

Clara S. Lewis is a senior lecturer at Dartmouth College. She is the author of *Tough on Hate? The Cultural Politics of Hate Crimes* and serves as an expert witness for neonaticide cases. She is also Mars and Ivy's mom.

Available titles in the Critical Issues in Crime and Society series:

Laura S. Abrams and Ben Anderson-Nathe, *Compassionate Confinement: A Year in the Life of Unit C*

Laura S. Abrams and Diane J. Terry, *Everyday Desistance: The Transition to Adulthood among Formerly Incarcerated Youth*

Tammy L. Anderson, ed., *Neither Villain nor Victim: Empowerment and Agency among Women Substance Abusers*

Miriam Boeri, *Women on Ice: Methamphetamine Use among Suburban Women*

Christian L. Bolden, *Out of the Red: My Life of Gangs, Prison, and Redemption*

Scott A. Bonn, *Mass Deception: Moral Panic and the U.S. War on Iraq*

Mary Bosworth and Jeanne Flavin, eds., *Race, Gender, and Punishment: From Colonialism to the War on Terror*

Henry H. Brownstein, Timothy M. Mulcahy, and Johannes Huessy, *The Methamphetamine Industry in America: Transnational Cartels and Local Entrepreneurs*

Ben Brucato, *Race and Police: The Origin of Our Peculiar Institutions*

Loretta Capeheart and Dragan Milovanovic, *Social Justice: Theories, Issues, and Movements*, Revised and expanded edition

Kim Cook, *Shattered Justice: Crime Victims' Experiences with Wrongful Convictions and Exonerations*

Alexandra Cox, *Trapped in a Vice: The Consequences of Confinement for Young People*

Anna Curtis, *Dangerous Masculinity: Fatherhood, Race, and Security inside America's Prisons*

Hilary Cuthrell, Luke Muentner, and Julie Poehlmann, *When Are You Coming Home? How Young Children Cope When Parents Go to Jail*

Walter S. DeKeseredy and Martin D. Schwartz, *Dangerous Exits: Escaping Abusive Relationships in Rural America*

Patricia E. Erickson and Steven K. Erickson, *Crime, Punishment, and Mental Illness: Law and the Behavioral Sciences in Conflict*

Jamie J. Fader, *Falling Back: Incarceration and Transitions to Adulthood among Urban Youth*

Luis A. Fernandez, *Policing Dissent: Social Control and the Anti-Globalization Movement*

Angela J. Hattery and Earl Smith, *Way Down in the Hole: Race, Intimacy, and the Reproduction of Racial Ideologies in Solitary Confinement*

Mike King, *When Riot Cops Are Not Enough: The Policing and Repression of Occupy Oakland*

Ronald C. Kramer, *Apocalyptic Crimes: Why Nuclear Weapons Are Illegal and Must Be Abolished*
Ronald C. Kramer, *Carbon Criminals, Climate Crimes*
Timothy R. Lauger, *Real Gangstas: Legitimacy, Reputation, and Violence in the Intergang Environment*
Margaret Leigey, *The Forgotten Men: Serving a Life without Parole Sentence*
Andrea Leverentz, *The Ex-Prisoner's Dilemma: How Women Negotiate Competing Narratives of Reentry and Desistance*
Ethan Czuy Levine, *Rape by the Numbers: Producing and Contesting Scientific Knowledge about Sexual Violence*
Clara S. Lewis, *American Infanticide: Sexism, Science, and the Politics of Sympathy*
Clara S. Lewis, *Tough on Hate? The Cultural Politics of Hate Crimes*
Michael J. Lynch, *Big Prisons, Big Dreams: Crime and the Failure of America's Penal System*
Erik S. Maloney and Kevin A. Wright, *Imprisoned Minds: Lost Boys, Trapped Men, and Solutions from Within the Prison*
Liam Martin, *The Social Logic of Recidivism: Cultural Capital from Prisons to the Streets*
Allison McKim, *Addicted to Rehab: Race, Gender, and Drugs in the Era of Mass Incarceration*
Raymond J. Michalowski and Ronald C. Kramer, eds., *State-Corporate Crime: Wrongdoing at the Intersection of Business and Government*
Susan L. Miller, *Victims as Offenders: The Paradox of Women's Violence in Relationships*
Torin Monahan, *Surveillance in the Time of Insecurity*
Torin Monahan and Rodolfo D. Torres, eds., *Schools under Surveillance: Cultures of Control in Public Education*
Ana Muñiz, *Police, Power, and the Production of Racial Boundaries*
Marianne O. Nielsen and Linda M. Robyn, *Colonialism Is Crime*
Leslie Paik, *Discretionary Justice: Looking Inside a Juvenile Drug Court*
Yasser Arafat Payne, Brooklynn Hitchens, and Darryl L. Chambers, *Murder Town, USA:*
Homicide, Structural Violence, and Activism
Anthony M. Platt, *The Child Savers: The Invention of Delinquency*, 40th anniversary edition with an introduction and critical commentaries compiled by Miroslava Chávez-García
Lois Presser, *Why We Harm*
Joshua M. Price, *Prison and Social Death*

Heidi Reynolds-Stenson, *Cultures of Resistance: Collective Action and Rationality in the Anti-Terror Age*

Diana Rickard, *Sex Offenders, Stigma, and Social Control*

Jeffrey Ian Ross, ed., *The Globalization of Supermax Prisons*

Dawn L. Rothe and Christopher W. Mullins, eds., *State Crime, Current Perspectives*

Jodi Schorb, *Reading Prisoners: Literature, Literacy, and the Transformation of American Punishment, 1700–1845*

Corinne Schwarz, *Policing Victimhood: Human Trafficking, Frontline Work, and the Carceral State*

Susan F. Sharp, *Hidden Victims: The Effects of the Death Penalty on Families of the Accused*

Susan F. Sharp, *Mean Lives, Mean Laws: Oklahoma's Women Prisoners*

Robert H. Tillman and Michael L. Indergaard, *Pump and Dump: The Rancid Rules of the New Economy*

Mariana Valverde, *Law and Order: Images, Meanings, Myths*

Michael Welch, *Crimes of Power and States of Impunity: The U.S. Response to Terror*

Michael Welch, *Scapegoats of September 11th: Hate Crimes and State Crimes in the War on Terror*

Saundra D. Westervelt and Kimberly J. Cook, *Life after Death Row: Exonerees' Search for Community and Identity*